ALCHEMY of
LOVE RELATIONSHIPS

ALCHEMY OF LOVE RELATIONSHIPS

A guide for using spiritual and metaphysical principles to heal the heart and create a lasting and loving relationship

JOSEPH MICHAEL LEVRY

Rootlight, Inc.
NEW YORK, NY

Rootlight, Inc.
15 Park Avenue Suite 7C
New York, NY 10016
www.rootlight.com

COVER AND TEXT DESIGN: Renée Skuba
PHOTOGRAPHY: Fredric Reschew, Mark Finne,
Marni Lustig, Pauline St. Denis
MODELS: Taunya Black, Noemie Ditzler,
Alyssa Gaustad, Renata Spironello

Printed in the United States of America
for Worldwide Distribution
ISBN 1-885562-27-6
Library of Congress Control Number: 00-090806

Also by Joseph Michael Levry

The Divine Doctor: Healing Beyond Medicine

The Healing Fire of Heaven
(previously titled *The Splendor of The Sun*)

Lifting the Veil: The Divine Code

CONTENTS

ACKNOWLEDGMENTS

This book is dedicated with love to my family; my mother, a constant source of strength; my sisters for their loving support; and especially Yannick for his healing optimism and sense of humor. I wish to express my love and gratitude to Yogi Bhajan, master of White Tantric and Kundalini yoga. Some of the meditations included in this book originate from his teachings.

I would also like to thank Hortense Dodo PhD, Gururattan Kaur Khalsa PhD, Carol Ann Saikhon, Teran Davis, Renée Skuba, Lynda "Tara" Guber, Ryan Rayston, Sabra Petersmann, Toni Patillo, plus many others for their assistance, input, and undying support of this work. My deepest gratitude goes to those who have helped me organize, edit, and produce *Alchemy of Love Relationships*. Without their labors of love, this book would not have come together with such ease.

This book was born out of the guidance and inspiration of the Benevolent Beings of Light who often teach me in my dreams. Knowing that we all have some form of challenging patterns, the last thing I wanted to do was pose as an expert on a subject so vast and complex as love relationships. I am grateful for their persistence and feel privileged to have been chosen to pass on their heavenly wisdom. It is my sincere desire that this work brings hope and joy to many.

Alchemy of Love Relationships was written to provide you with tools for self-healing and protection. Let your being absorb its sacred wisdom, so that you may be guided through the complex situations of love and life. While many books have been written on love relationships, tantric sex, and the physiology of sex, none have dealt with these topics in such an enlightening way. The principles offered in the *Alchemy of Love Relationships*, however, take the nature of love relationship to a higher dimension. Use them, and they will change the way you view and engage in love and life.

I have found the principles revealed herein to be both accurate and extremely helpful. I am confident that genuine knowledge of these truths, in combination with their practical application, will prove to be of great value to every man or woman who desires to build, nurture, and maintain a healthy love relationship. At the core of these truths, which have never before been made public, are the unseen forces of nature that direct every relationship. Ignorance of their existence and relevance is the disease that shortens the life span of relationships and bitterly breaks the heart. Therefore, it is vital for love partners to take the time to examine the ways in which the powerful forces of nature are at work. Knowing the implications and applications of these forces, coupled with personal responsibility, provides you with a foundation from which to act in regards to your love life. As you engage in your love relationship with increased knowledge, you will discover that you now have a wealth of options at your fingertips that allow you to respond and act in nurturing and healthy ways.

Take these timeless gems of wisdom and priceless pearls of knowledge, and feed yourself. Allow them to enlighten and brighten your love relationship. If you and your partner remain open to these sacred teachings, they will fill your hearts and inspire your minds to reach new depths of understanding. Allow these principles to become the beacon of light that steers you through the shadows of love towards the ultimate potential future that is your divine birthright and destiny. They will transform your love relationship into a spiritual journey of self-healing whereby each aspect of trans-formation is embraced as new gifts are discovered. Indeed, this spiritual journey becomes a wonderful opportunity for each partner to discern the parts of himself or herself that exist in an imbalanced state. Then, through the power of their own conscious understand-ing of the truth, these imbalances can be corrected.

JOSEPH MICHAEL LEVRY
New York City • 2004

Introduction

Many books on love have been published in the last century, but none provides a detailed account of the laws governing love. *The Alchemy of Love Relationships* is an original and entirely unique book on relationships, because it explains the dynamics of romantic partnerships and gives us a deep understanding of the nature and needs of individual souls. Many relationships end when, instead of clearing the path for peace and happiness, unaware couples accidentally create more karma, miscommunication, pain, and struggle.

The *Alchemy of Love Relationships* reveals how to use the birth dates of a couple to apply facets of divine spiritual wisdom, the Hebrew alphabet, tarot, and astrology to illuminate the dynamic of their soul paths. These spiritual laws, which have never before been made public, are the unseen forces that direct every relationship. This book gives us specific formulas for achieving successful and satisfying unions. Best of all, it instructs us on how to actively apply this knowledge to lift intimate relationships from a casual state to a divine one.

This book will also reveal simple, practical and time-proven spiritual principles that will provide you with the necessary skills to find a partner right for you. I have also added meditations and simple exercises from Kundalini yoga. These are specifically designed to enhance your health, balance the mind and body, develop your intuition, and nourish your energy as your spirit opens to the ancient wisdom of the alchemy of love.

I am confident that applying the spiritual insights revealed in this book can largely decrease the number of unnecessary heartbreaks and divorces, clearing the way for divinity and grace to inhabit your love life. The *Alchemy of Love Relationships* will help you understand the soul essence of your mate and yourself.

From childhood, I knew that the universe had graciously blessed me with an innate knowledge of the ancient secret wisdom of the Kabbalah. As a result, I feel compelled to teach, counsel and heal others by imparting and applying this expedient wisdom. This has led me to many places throughout the world. During my extensive travels all over the USA, Europe, and Asia, I have met interesting people from all walks of life—from the poorest slum dwellers to the richest corporate executives. As I counseled them during their travails, I soon discovered a common thread: that love, or the lack of it, was the focus of most of their troubles. I diligently recorded and spent much time scrupulously analyzing all my findings, a process which allowed me, in quiet retrospect, to track and accurately predict the day, month and year for marriage. Invariably, I was struck to find that every person's troubles could be attributed to one simple thing: deeply rooted subconscious psychic patterns.

The explanation for this phenomenon, although ancient, is simple: All that is said and done is retained forever in the Akashic records. Nothing is ever lost nor forgotten. Although each of us has led many, often completely different lives, we incarnate at birth each time still carrying the past burdens of our unresolved karma—our accrued emotional debts and unresolved entanglements—in order to work them through to their proper natural and spiritual conclusions. To draw a metaphysical parallel, we are like the Sun, which rises each day at dawn, reaches its zenith at noon, and sets at night. Like the Sun we are born, grow to maturity, then decline toward death. To continue the metaphor further, just as sunset occurs at one location and sunrise at another, so does our death in this location—the physical world of Earth—become our rebirth in another—the astral world of the spirit.

After death, our soul follows its compulsion by the laws of the astral world to reincarnate in a physical body to achieve a balance of its karmic debts. Meanwhile, all the memories of our former lives on Earth remain buried in our subconscious mind, and these memories constitute those deeply rooted subconscious psychic patterns that remain imprinted before our incarnation on Earth.

There are some people who, no matter how successful or beautiful they may be, never seem to attract the right mate. There are others who cannot stay in a relationship for very long. Unless you go to the root of your relationship problems, it is difficult to completely resolve them.

Negative energy patterns written in one's aura can produce a blueprint for recurring unhealthy relationships. Those patterns act like a "negative" from which photographs are reproduced. Even if you destroy the photographs, you do not change the negative. In other words, men and women go from relationship to relationship hoping for a miracle, but end up in similar circumstances. Unfortunately, those patterns which attract unhealthy relationships are still present, keeping many of us in a self-destructive loop. These very patterns cause people to experience verbal, emotional, physical, sexual or even financial abuse at the hands of those they love. Therefore, what is so vital to finding the right relationship is to eliminate those patterns that produce unhealthy unions. Otherwise, getting divorced will continue to be as common as changing socks, and the remains of the failed relationships will continue to litter every city and town.

I am going to reveal some important points now. These psychic patterns come from seven specific sources:

The first source is our debts from past lives.
The second source is our father.
The third source is our mother.
The fourth source is our mother's womb.
The fifth source is our upbringing.
The sixth source is our environment.
The seventh source is the Kabbalistic planet ruling our birthday.

To summarize, we first must naturally consider our debts from past lives, called *karma*—what we already carry into this physical world at birth. Second and third, there is the hard fact of our parentage. When our father's sperm unites with our mother's ovum to form the first cell, or *zygote*, the unity of their own repertories of genes creates a new gene pool in us. Scientifically speaking, the zygote carries and imparts both gene patterns of our mother and our father as the blueprint—or vehicle—with which we incarnate on this Earth. Therefore, some of the patterns I am discussing here are inherited. This explains why, if either or both parents are abusive, the children will exhibit a strong propensity towards abusive behavior or attract an abusive partner. This genetic transference of patterns applies as well for children whose parents are alcoholics, drug addicts or suicidal. Moreover, if one of the parents fled the home, the adult child also will tend to flee from relationships, whether or not he or she initiated the relationship.

Continuing our discussion on the sources of subconscious patterns, the fourth source of these patterns is the environment of your mother's womb. That is where all the idiosyncratic likes, dislikes, hopes, fears and anxieties of your mother become an intrinsic part of your psyche.

The fifth source is the way your parents raised you, most specifically between the ages of one to eleven. It is in this manner that all the negative and positive conditioning took place, and remains in effect today. All those old familiar patterns of frustration, fear, wounds, embarrassment and anger that plague us as adults happened during those crucial years.

The sixth source is your environment. For example, some of us who were raised in an abusive environment may grow up thinking that abuse is acceptable. This is how the environment becomes a part of the pattern.

Thus, we can easily see how every single experience we undergo leaves an imprint on our psyches. The intensity of each experience, whether it is joy, sadness or pain, will determine the force of the imprint. These imprints will become seedbeds in which our thoughts and actions bloom and grow, becoming the garden of our present and future experiences. Furthermore, the mind is like a computer: all it knows is what has been programmed into its memory. Therefore, when the mind is confronted with a new situation, it retrieves the data necessary to process the commands from the program of our past experiences. All relationships subsequent to our primary ones and those we formed long ago with family members will always engender the same reactions. That is because the mind, a creature of habit, likes to attach itself to old, familiar patterns since that is all it knows. That psychological conditioning is made up of our likes, dislikes, prejudices, frustrations, negative human qualities, attitudes, habits, experiences, regrets, fears, anger, anxieties, guilt, shame, and much, much more. Therefore, our subconscious urges keep us forever in a loop consisting of the past experiences of our conscious mind, which are the real obstacles to happiness.

The seventh and final source of subconscious patterns is the Kabbalistic planet that rules the days surrounding your birthday. The vibrations of that planet will affect you from the cradle to the grave. The planets are seven in number and the days of the week have been named after them. In their order from Sunday through Saturday they stand for the Sun, Moon, Mars, Mercury, Jupiter, Venus, and Saturn. They may have a positive or negative impact on you. For example, if you were born on Sunday, you will be ruled by the Sun, which is the fountain of life. You may display the positive pattern of brilliancy or the negative pattern of boastfulness. If you were born on Monday, ruled by the Moon—the planet of dreams and imagination—you could be either intuitive or moody and selfish. If Mars—the planet of war—is your ruling planet, you will be either energetic or aggressive. A person born on Wednesday will be ruled by Mercury—the planet of communication. On the positive side, this person would display eloquence, and on the negative side, he or she would be dishonest. Jupiter rules Thursday and is the planet of material wellness. It may make you either ambitious and a leader or dominating. Venus, the planet of love, affection and passion, rules Friday. This planet will make you either graceful and romantic or promiscuous. Finally, the last planet is Saturn—the lord of karma. Saturn could make you spiritual and disciplined or melancholic.

It is vital that you familiarize yourself with the seven creative planets, particularly the one that rules your day of birth. These planets are the door to your happiness. Understanding their influence will allow you to become the master of your life.

The holy Kabbalah is the key to the mysteries of creation. Astrology, numerology, tarot cards and palmistry all come from the Kabbalah. According to it, God created the universe based upon the following numeric patterns of 3 – 7 – 12. This pattern is based upon the 22 letters of the Hebrew alphabet. It has its correspondences in time, space and humanity. No one can really change time. The only thing one can really do is change space to improve one's destiny. The understanding of space constitutes one of the greatest secrets in mastering the unseen forces.

The planet that rules your birthday is your master key. Although there are various ways of finding out the day of the week you were born, I recommend that you consult the chart on the following page or an ephemeris.

As previously mentioned, there are both positive and negative aspects to each of the planetary energies. If you live consciously, you will most likely manifest the positive aspects, whereas an unconscious life will express the negative qualities. Just remember that your destructive patterns will often manifest through the negative aspects of the planet that rules your day of birth. Therefore, the following information will be very useful.

I am giving this in order for love mates to know as much about their partner and themselves as they can. I have seen so many failed relationships, where had the partners possessed even the slightest knowledge of the positive and negative aspects revealed by their planet, their love union may have been saved. I felt it a duty to include in this book the indications of character and tendencies, which may be easily learned by knowing the planet which rules one's day of birth. I believe that knowledge of the positive and negative aspects of the ruling planet is not only useful, but even essential if one wishes to succeed in creating a joyful love life. Love partners who learn more about their planet and their partner's will certainly be thrice-armed in battling unhealthy patterns, and consequently move the relationship to a healthy and harmonious space.

Guide to Determine Day of Birth

STEP I: Select year desired, obtain letter as key.

STEP 2: With key and month desired, obtain number of true month.

STEP 3: With true month number and day desired, determine the day of the week.

EXAMPLE: *Day desired is July 20, 1903.*

I) **Key** is *H.* 2) **True Month** is *15.* 3) **Day** is *Monday.*

STEP I: Obtain key for selected year

CALENDAR FROM 1881 TO 2008

1881 J	1900 N	1919 L	1938 J	1957 K	1976 F	1995 M
1882 M	1901 K	1920 F	1939 M	1958 L	1977 J	1996 D
1883 N	1902 L	1921 J	1940 D	1959 H	1978 M	1997 L
1884 G	1903 H	1922 M	1941 L	1960 B	1979 N	1998 H
1885 H	1904 B	1923 N	1942 H	1961 M	1980 G	1999 I
1886 I	1905 M	1924 G	1943 I	1962 N	1981 H	2000 E
1887 J	1906 N	1925 H	1944 E	1963 K	1982 I	2001 N
1888 A	1907 K	1926 I	1945 N	1964 C	1983 J	2002 K
1889 K	1908 C	1927 J	1946 K	1965 I	1984 A	2003 L
1890 L	1909 I	1928 A	1947 L	1966 J	1985 K	2004 F
1891 H	1910 J	1929 K	1948 F	1967 M	1986 L	2005 J
1892 B	1911 M	1930 L	1949 J	1968 D	1987 H	2006 M
1893 M	1912 D	1931 H	1950 M	1969 L	1988 B	2007 N
1894 N	1913 L	1932 B	1951 N	1970 H	1989 M	2008 G
1895 K	1914 H	1933 M	1952 G	1971 I	1990 N	
1896 C	1915 I	1934 N	1953 H	1972 E	1991 K	
1897 I	1916 E	1935 K	1954 I	1973 N	1992 C	
1898 J	1917 N	1936 C	1955 J	1974 K	1993 I	
1899 M	1918 K	1937 I	1956 A	1975 L	1994 J	

STEP 2: Use key to obtain True Month

Leap Years

	A	B	C	D	E	F	G
JAN	18	20	15	17	19	14	16
FEB	1	3	12	28	2	4	27
MAR	14	16	18	20	15	17	19
APRIL	25	13	22	24	26	21	23
MAY	16	18	20	15	17	19	14
JUNE	13	22	24	26	21	23	25
JULY	18	20	15	17	19	14	16
AUG	15	17	19	14	16	18	20
SEPT	26	21	23	25	13	22	24
OCT	17	19	14	16	18	20	15
NOV	21	23	25	13	22	24	26
DEC	19	14	16	18	20	15	17
	A	B	C	D	E	F	G

Common Years

	H	I	J	K	L	M	N
JAN	14	20	19	16	15	18	17
FEB	11	10	9	6	5	8	7
MAR	18	17	16	20	19	15	14
APRIL	22	21	13	24	23	26	25
MAY	20	19	18	15	14	17	16
JUNE	24	23	22	26	25	21	13
JULY	15	14	20	17	16	19	18
AUG	19	18	17	14	20	16	15
SEPT	23	22	21	25	24	13	26
OCT	14	20	19	16	15	18	17
NOV	25	24	23	13	26	22	21
DEC	16	15	14	18	17	20	19
	H	I	J	K	L	M	N

STEP 3: Obtain day of the week

			No. 1			
Su	M	T	W	Th	F	Sa
			1	2	3	4
5	6	7	8	9	10	11
12	13	14	15	16	17	18
19	20	21	22	23	24	25
26	27	28	29			

			No. 2			
Su	M	T	W	Th	F	Sa
		1	2	3	4	5
6	7	8	9	10	11	12
13	14	15	16	17	18	19
20	21	22	23	24	25	26
27	28	29				

			No. 3			
Su	M	T	W	Th	F	Sa
	1	2	3	4	5	6
7	8	9	10	11	12	13
14	15	16	17	18	19	20
21	22	23	24	25	26	27
28	29					

			No. 4			
Su	M	T	W	Th	F	Sa
1	2	3	4	5	6	7
8	9	10	11	12	13	14
15	16	17	18	19	20	21
22	23	24	25	26	27	28
29						

			No. 5			
Su	M	T	W	Th	F	Sa
						1
2	3	4	5	6	7	8
9	10	11	12	13	14	15
16	17	18	19	20	21	22
23	24	25	26	27	28	

			No. 6			
Su	M	T	W	Th	F	Sa
					1	2
3	4	5	6	7	8	9
10	11	12	13	14	15	16
17	18	19	20	21	22	23
24	25	26	27	28		

			No. 7			
Su	M	T	W	Th	F	Sa
				1	2	3
4	5	6	7	8	9	10
11	12	13	14	15	16	17
18	19	20	21	22	23	24
25	26	27	28			

			No. 8			
Su	M	T	W	Th	F	Sa
		1	2	3	4	
5	6	7	8	9	10	11
12	13	14	15	16	17	18
19	20	21	22	23	24	25
26	27	28				

			No. 9			
Su	M	T	W	Th	F	Sa
	1	2	3	4	5	
6	7	8	9	10	11	12
13	14	15	16	17	18	19
20	21	22	23	24	25	26
27	28					

			No. 10			
Su	M	T	W	Th	F	Sa
	1	2	3	4	5	6
7	8	9	10	11	12	13
14	15	16	17	18	19	20
21	22	23	24	25	26	27
28						

			No. 11			
Su	M	T	W	Th	F	Sa
1	2	3	4	5	6	7
8	9	10	11	12	13	14
15	16	17	18	19	20	21
22	23	24	25	26	27	28

			No. 12			
Su	M	T	W	Th	F	Sa
						1
2	3	4	5	6	7	8
9	10	11	12	13	14	15
16	17	18	19	20	21	22
23	24	25	26	27	28	29

			No. 13			
Su	M	T	W	Th	F	Sa
					1	2
3	4	5	6	7	8	9
10	11	12	13	14	15	16
17	18	19	20	21	22	23
24	25	26	27	28	29	30

			No. 14			
Su	M	T	W	Th	F	Sa
				1	2	3
4	5	6	7	8	9	10
11	12	13	14	15	16	17
18	19	20	21	22	23	24
25	26	27	28	29	30	31

			No. 15			
Su	M	T	W	Th	F	Sa
		1	2	3	4	
5	6	7	8	9	10	11
12	13	14	15	16	17	18
19	20	21	22	23	24	25
26	27	28	29	30	31	

No. 16

Su	M	T	W	Th	F	Sa
		1	2	3	4	5
6	7	8	9	10	11	12
13	14	15	16	17	18	19
20	21	22	23	24	25	26
27	28	29	30	31		

No. 17

Su	M	T	W	Th	F	Sa
	1	2	3	4	5	6
7	8	9	10	11	12	13
14	15	16	17	18	19	20
21	22	23	24	25	26	27
28	29	30	31			

No. 18

Su	M	T	W	Th	F	Sa
1	2	3	4	5	6	7
8	9	10	11	12	13	14
15	16	17	18	19	20	21
22	23	24	25	26	27	28
29	30	31				

No. 19

Su	M	T	W	Th	F	Sa
						1
2	3	4	5	6	7	8
9	10	11	12	13	14	15
16	17	18	19	20	21	22
23	24	25	26	27	28	29
30	31					

No. 20

Su	M	T	W	Th	F	Sa
					1	2
3	4	5	6	7	8	9
10	11	12	13	14	15	16
17	18	19	20	21	22	23
24	25	26	27	28	29	30
31						

No. 21

Su	M	T	W	Th	F	Sa
				1	2	3
4	5	6	7	8	9	10
11	12	13	14	15	16	17
18	19	20	21	22	23	24
25	26	27	28	29	30	

No. 22

Su	M	T	W	Th	F	Sa
		1	2	3	4	
5	6	7	8	9	10	11
12	13	14	15	16	17	18
19	20	21	22	23	24	25
26	27	28	29	30		

No. 23

Su	M	T	W	Th	F	Sa
	1	2	3	4	5	
6	7	8	9	10	11	12
13	14	15	16	17	18	19
20	21	22	23	24	25	26
27	28	29	30			

No. 24

Su	M	T	W	Th	F	Sa
	1	2	3	4	5	6
7	8	9	10	11	12	13
14	15	16	17	18	19	20
21	22	23	24	25	26	27
28	29	30				

No. 25

Su	M	T	W	Th	F	Sa
1	2	3	4	5	6	7
8	9	10	11	12	13	14
15	16	17	18	19	20	21
22	23	24	25	26	27	28
29	30					

No. 26

Su	M	T	W	Th	F	Sa
						1
2	3	4	5	6	7	8
9	10	11	12	13	14	15
16	17	18	19	20	21	22
23	24	25	26	27	28	29
30						

No. 27

Su	M	T	W	Th	F	Sa
					1	2
3	4	5	6	7	8	9
10	11	12	13	14	15	16
17	18	19	20	21	22	23
24	25	26	27	28	29	

No. 28

Su	M	T	W	Th	F	Sa
				1	2	3
4	5	6	7	8	9	10
11	12	13	14	15	16	17
18	19	20	21	22	23	24
25	26	27	28	29		

The Days of the Week and the Ruling Planets

DAY	RULING PLANET
Sunday	Sun
Monday	Moon
Tuesday	Mars
Wednesday	Mercury
Thursday	Jupiter
Friday	Venus
Saturday	Saturn

Sun

The Sun stands for spirituality, divinity, health and wealth. The Sun gives you highly creative energy. This aspect gives you all the courage, confidence, will and self-love it takes to be successful in your endeavors. The Sun makes you ambitious, proud and generous. Sun people love to be the center of attention. You are outgoing and warm. Avoid becoming too self-involved and domineering. Those born with the Sun often leave their mark behind in the world.

Positive: Generous, warm-hearted and loving.
Negative: Dominating, impractical and irresponsible.

Moon

The Moon rules the realm of imagination, dreams and family life. It is the planet of imagination and the subconscious. It makes you very emotional. In other words, you feel your way through life. You often fluctuate, thus making decisions difficult. You are dreamy and benefit psychologically by being around water. People born under the vibration of the Moon can amass great wealth, but they have a hard time holding on to it, because they like to spend and give. It is very important to develop a healthy sense of giving, and be aware of over-identification and over-attachments.

Positive: Intuitive, compassionate and cooperative.

Negative: Secretive, self-centered and procrastinating.

Mars

Mars rules physical energy, war and initiative. Mars represents ambition, energy, courage and transformation. It gives you great strength of individuality and independence. This vibration produces a person who is action-oriented and has an abundance of energy. Mars people can be outspoken and dictative in their behavior, which can create distressing conditions in domestic life. The challenging aspect of Mars represents war, internal and external struggles, desire, impulse and aggression. It can make one abrupt and possibly reckless. A person with Mars can not get away with impulsive, irresponsible behavior, because they learn the hard way. Therefore, it is best to think before acting, rather than acting or speaking on impulse. There is a tendency for quick emotional flare-ups, which usually dissipate as quickly as they arise. The greatest challenge is to relax.

Positive: Energetic, loyal and magnetic.

Negative: Aggressive, quarrelsome and vindictive.

Mercury

Mercury rules communication, health and the mind. It also stands for perception and intellect. It will give you an incredibly active, logical and analytical mind, and a canny ability to see the humor and absurd side of situations. Mercury will also give you a quick mind and a special way with words. You can excel in all forms of communication, and will do well dealing with information. It is very important to avoid worrying and learn to relax.

Positive: Adaptable, eloquent and intelligent.

Negative: Dishonest, changeable and superficial.

Jupiter

Jupiter rules material and spiritual richness. It is the lord of abundance. Jupiter is in charge of health, fortune, success, prosperity, and happiness. It is known as The Lord of Lords—the greatest of all planets. It rules expansion, travel, justice, religion, higher values and morality. Your fair and diplomatic ways are attributed to Jupiter. Spirituality will stimulate your interest. You will benefit from anything that is expansive, especially travel. Your warmth and generosity will open doors for you. You need to maintain moderation when it comes to food.

Positive: Straightforward, sociable and optimistic.

Negative: Intolerant, bossy and temperamental.

Venus

Venus rules harmony, beauty, romance and sexual pleasures. It rules art, music, dance, theater, beauty, luxury and fashion. Although you may not be an artist yourself, Venus will give you love and appreciation for art and aesthetics. You are concerned with luxury, sensuality, and social affairs. Venus can make you very romantic and often a bit indulgent. You may like to decorate, design, and beautify yourself and your surroundings. Venus gives you refinement and a sense of style. It can make you graceful and sociable. You should avoid being vain, promiscuous, unfaithful, inconstant or overly materialistic. Many of your challenges in life will come through relationships with the opposite sex.

Positive: Gentle, graceful and sociable.

Negative: Promiscuous, vain and vacillating.

Saturn

Saturn, the lord of karma, stands for balance, order, reason, stability and knowledge. Saturn is also the planet of discipline, rules, laws, limitations and obstacles. Saturn's energy is contractive. It is related to organization, structure, responsibility, ambition and perseverance. It will give you an organizing mind and make you a master of structure and form. It requires caution, restraint, focus and concentration.

You are strengthened by challenge and persistence. Avoid being melancholic or overly authoritative; learn to laugh and lighten up. You may experience delays, restriction, struggle, anxiety and fears that are unnecessary. Most great teachers are born under Saturn. A person with Saturn can not get away with frivolous, irresponsible behavior, because Saturn people pay for their actions and learn the hard way. Therefore, it is important to lead a clean life.

Positive: Good morality, trustworthy and stable.

Negative: Fearful, withdrawn and melancholic.

Planetary Compatibility

The secrets of the unseen forces that direct our intimate relationships are hidden in the seven creative planets. As previously mentioned, your destructive patterns manifest through the negative aspects of the planets that rule your day of birth. Being aware of them allows you to move your relationship from negativity to positivity.

Let's take an example. If you were born on a Friday—ruled by Venus—your negative tendencies will cause you to be promiscuous, vain and vacillating. Those aspects will be very damaging to your relationship. On the contrary, by being gentle, graceful and sociable, you can help create a platform for a fulfilling relationship. For a partner born on a Tuesday—ruled by Mars—he or she will need to avoid being aggressive, quarrelsome and vindictive. On the other hand, his energy, loyalty and magnetism will be very constructive to the love union.

Here's another example where one partner was born on Wednesday and the other on Saturday. They are respectively ruled by Mercury and Saturn. Let's say the Mercury person is dishonest, changeable and superficial in this relationship, and the Saturn person is fearful, withdrawn and melancholic. It is obvious that such a relationship will never last, because both partners are setting themselves up for abuse.

Remember that as the negative aspects weaken your love relationship, so do the positive ones strengthen and nurture both partners. All you need is your partner's birthday in order to know what you are getting into.

CHAPTER ONE

Principle of Causality

All of our early childhood experiences registered in our psyches' memory banks become the most powerful influences in our lives. They shape our attitudes and beliefs and affect the present. They keep us in duplicity and out of reality. They make many of us afraid to bring these old experiences into conscious awareness, so that we can more easily analyze and thus neutralize them. Quite simply, they are the only things preventing us from enjoying healthy relationships. Our liberation from the cycle of unhappy relationships will only happen when we start becoming aware of those patterns. In order for us to liberate ourselves from those negative karmic influences, we must accept total responsibility for facing them. This is not an easy thing to do, but it must be done. Those undesirable negative karmic influences or bad habits are not only stored in the deeper parts of the mind, but are also our worst enemies. Since our lives follow those patterns, they stay with us from one incarnation to the next until they are fully resolved. Therefore, the only way out is to face them now rather than later. Otherwise they will become unresolved conflicts engendering neurotic symptoms, such as the neural disorders of psychological stress.

Humanity is a product of spiritual forces: we come by the spirit, live by the spirit, and go by the spirit. If we admit that life is very spiritual, it is logical to assume that love relationships are also spiritual. Therefore, common sense dictates that the application of mystical wisdom in creating a stable relationship is the best solution for modern men and women confronted by various psychological pressures.

Simply stated, being spiritual means being aware. Spiritual living is conscious living. Conscious living brings happiness, for it allows us to merge harmoniously with the principle of causality, the immutable law which dictates the experiences of every man and woman. Thus, it would be illogical not to admit that the law of cause and effect affects our lives, or to deny its effects on our love relationships.

Don't worry, because there is nothing scary about this law! It is a law known directly or indirectly by all, but neglected by most. It is so simple and trivial-sounding, yet when truly understood and intelligently applied, it can be most powerful and rewarding. It only gets the best of you when you ignore it! But if you work with it, it becomes your ally and assists you in all your endeavors, and most especially in your love relationships.

Allow me to expand on this law:

For every hour of pain that you cause,
for every moment of grief that you bring upon someone,
you shall also suffer,
now in this life, or in the next reincarnation.
For every evil thought, you shall suffer accordingly.
For every destructive thought,
you shall be reduced accordingly.
But for every good deed,
you will be compensated with a good deed done to you.
For every constructive thought or act,
you shall be rejuvenated and uplifted.
For every gift,
you shall reap a return in goodness.
All things shall be equalized,
not at some distant time,
but at the setting of each Sun,
at the ticking of each passing second.
Nothing is ever lost. Nothing is ever forgotten.

When you begin a sequence of events you will someday have to face the consequences of the actions taken. That is the law of nature! If you cause someone to unjustly suffer, the punishment, which is the effect of that cause, will come to you within seven years.

The number seven is a very spiritual number. It corresponds to the seven creative planets. (These will be expanded upon in later chapters). The payback of the karmic debt can last anywhere between three and ten years! Similarly, if you help someone to be happy, your reward, which is the effect, will come to you within seven years and may last between three and seven years.

Therefore, to avoid tragic consequences, you have to control the sequence from the beginning. Quite simply: *to avoid a reaction, control the action.*

The big question is, of course, how can one know the consequences before one even starts the sequence? God gave free will to all of us to use in making decisions every day. Every second of our lives is a new challenge fraught with difficult choices. Bad choices make us suffer; good choices bring us happiness. How can one know that the marriage he or she is entering into today will not end in a painful divorce years from now? The answer is through intuitively adhering to those ancient and immutable principles revealed to you in this book.

Let me begin with a discussion of two important planets, Saturn and Jupiter. Saturn, as the Lord of Karma, stands for discipline and balance. It is the teacher. When you perform bad actions, it is Saturn's reciprocal power that will exact your punishment. Jupiter, on the other hand, is the Lord of Material Wellness, and as such will reward those who perform beneficial acts. When you operate from duality, Saturn teaches you the hard way, whereas when you act from oneness, Jupiter will reward you. The key for us, then, is to move from duality to divinity. *There is no reality in duality, only confusion. Reality is pure Oneness.* There is no freedom from patterns within the duality of the mind. The only way to avoid the negative patterns is through moving from duality to divinity or Oneness. If you enter into a love relationship from a place of duality, you are likely to suffer later from a broken heart. Those who live in duality—

impetuously, heedlessly, unconsciously—are ruled by fluctuation. Sadly, this accounts for most of the human population! Those people always follow their heads, and the head is ruled by the Moon, which signifies fluctuation. Thus, unconscious living makes one useless and hopeless.

CHAPTER TWO

The Law of the Triangle

God is a trinity: Father, Son, and Holy Spirit. The number three represents an equilateral triangle—a symbol of perfection. Every manifestation in the material world follows the ancient law of the triangle: two opposites must unite to form a third condition of perfection. In the Kabbalistic Tree of Life, from Kether to Malkuth, most of the spheres are disposed to form triangles. These are called ternaries, which correspond to the different worlds, from Earth to Heaven.

Love relationships as well are based upon the law of the triangle. There are three triangles which represent the three gradations that every relationship must experience before becoming divine. For one moment, imagine an equilateral triangle with the apex down—the man is at the upper left point and the woman is at the upper right. At the lower point or apex, there is the condition that stabilizes the relationship. When physical intercourse is at the third point, the relationship remains at the first and lowest gradation. When communication is added to physical intercourse, we have the second gradation. Finally, the third gradation is when spirituality or God is at the third point.

The first gradation is ruled by the law of adhesion. It is motivated by physical attraction and sex. As I previously mentioned, this law of adhesion is the lowest grade of union. In other words, you can use glue to stick an apple and an orange together; they do not

necessarily have to be compatible. Those who behave and act unconsciously will remain in the lower gradation. Automatic living will
pull you toward this stage with someone with whom you are not
compatible. People who are sexual addicts, for example, are stuck at
that level. They operate from the sexual chakra only—sex is the only
way they can relate to another person. If you enter this point unconsciously, you will most likely suffer a broken heart and all types of
abuse. On the other hand, conscious living will keep you away from
all problematic unions because you live through intuition. The animalistic experience of the first gradation is never permanent, because
like everything in the physical world, it is ruled by change. The initial intensity of sexual desires eventually dissipates—the new
becomes old. When the novelty of physical intercourse (the third
point of the triangle) is gone, one needs to find another element to
maintain the probability of the love relationship.

In the second gradation, the love between the man and woman
must rest upon common goals and interests, such as children, art,
movies, traveling, etc. If art, for example, is the shared interest, it
becomes the third point and the triangle maintains its stability.
Although the sex continues, the relationship moves to the next level
of intercourse—communication.

The tongue, which represents the Sun, must go in intercourse
with the upper palate, or Moon, to create the sound of communication. Another form of intercourse in communication is speaking
and listening. Speaking is active and giving, representing the solar or
male energy. Listening is passive and receptive, representing the lunar
or female energy. Men and women must communicate openly and
honestly from the heart. When one speaks, the other must pay attention and listen and vice versa. It must be done with patience, respect
and love. If both speak at the same time, the fire of the Sun becomes
too hot and burns the relationship. If both stop talking and listen
at the same time, the coolness increases to freeze the relationship.
When speaking and listening alternate, then the law of balance
creates stability. If there is no communication after the initial excitement over sex is gone, the couple automatically grows apart. Some
couples stay at this level and consider themselves fairly happy.

There comes a point where the couple grows beyond the second gradation. They need another element to move the relationship to the divine state—the level of soul mate. This stage is ruled by the Law of Cohesion; it is the divine level. If you put two drops of water side by side, they form one drop. When the love between a woman and a man centers upon spirituality, it attracts the blessings of God.

When Divinity is the third point of the triangle, it moves the relationship from duality to Oneness. At the second gradation, movies, work, traveling are all material and physical—they are ruled by change and are never constant. God, however, never changes; He is constant and immutable. Concentrating on Divinity moves the relationship from the illusion of duality to the reality of Oneness. This is the relationship which can successfully overcome any challenge and survive indefinitely. This is when you know you have found your soul mate. Often this type of couple will find it easy to meditate and pray together, not needing to express themselves verbally. At this level, when one partner lives in another city or is traveling, the connection is still intact, strong as steel, beyond time and space, ruled by Light. It is Divine and in perfect harmony. Both partners receive love and healing energy from each other as all the gradations of the triangle are combined. There is no abuse, and trust is never an issue. Happiness is the gift of such a relationship, and the couple has the ability to heal all who come in contact with them. This uplifting kind of relationship is mental, spiritual and physical—what each of us strives to achieve.

Intuition is the powerful voice of the soul.
It is best described as an inner capability,
a latent potential to raise the consciousness
of the mind, so that one's perceptive
ability shifts, and one is able to accurately
perceive the truth beyond the illusion of reality.

CHAPTER THREE

Intuition and the Sixth Chakra

L ocated between the eyebrows, the sixth chakra is known as the third eye. It is the realm of projected truth, which is divine, infinite and safe, and the arena of projection and sophistication. It is the operation of solar, lunar and neutral currents. As our spiritual teacher and protector, the third eye relates to knowledge, wisdom and the development of intuition. It sees what our other two eyes cannot. When we meditate on the third eye, we stimulate the central nervous system. Our goal is to open the conscious third eye in order to accurately see what it is we need to do, receive, extend, expel and contract. The dominant concern of the sixth chakra is that we continue to raise our consciousness.

Allow me to clarify. The third eye does not see what appears to be, but rather it sees the unseen from which we have come and to which we will return. The difference between intuition and sight granted by the third eye and a psychic capacity is that intuition works on the cosmic energy given by the solar centers, while psychic ability works on the individual energy. A white magician acts as a humble instrument of God consciousness. A black magician acts as the servant of individual consciousness.

Intuition is the powerful voice of the soul. It tells us when something is working or not, and when someone is well-meaning or not. Intuition is best described as an inner capability, a latent potential to raise the consciousness of the mind, so that the perceptive ability of the individual shifts, and he is able to accurately perceive the truth beyond the illusion of reality. When this occurs, the individual is free from physical form and feeling. He is operating outside the bonds of time and space. His intuition understands less common truths and relays them back to the physical form, where they can be put to good use.

It is through intuition that we arrive at a point of neutral understanding whereby we see clearly. In every area of life, intuition gives us the ability to eliminate decisions based on trial and error. For example, a heightened level of intuition can prevent you from becoming involved in the wrong love relationship. Conversely, a heightened level of intuition can help you find the right love relationship. Remember, intuition is the quiet, internal voice of the soul that gives you an immediate sense of someone's character and motivations. Imagine then, how intuition becomes an important tool when choosing a mate. Upon meeting someone in a romantic context your intuition acts as a guide, subtly steering you either toward a joyful, positive experience, or away from a painful, negative experience. Surely if you think back over the course of your romantic life, you will find that your intuition told you certain truths about your romantic partners. How many of us have made statements like, "I knew in the beginning, but I stayed," or "I should have followed through with him/her, but I didn't." Statements such as these reflect moments in time when your intuition tried desperately to guide you in the right direction. Had you taken a moment to silence your rationalizing mind and listen to your intuition, you could have positively altered the course of your life. Keep in mind that life is not a gamble, and guesswork will only bring you pain. Nothing is ever left to chance. The universe itself was mathematically built, and has its own rhythm and flow.

Intuition is the force that opens us to receive knowledge from a plane of higher spiritual truths. When our intuition is fully active, we find answers to the mysteries of the universe. The unanswered questions that once burned inside our souls become as easy to decode as a children's book. We simply need to turn the key and unlock the door of our latent, intuitive capabilities.

Transcendence of the physical realm has been mastered and practiced for thousands of years by those who have allowed their consciousness to grow. Those who master the art of transcendence have developed their consciousness to the point where they are able to see beyond the illusions of the material world. Once the veil of illusion is lifted, the truth steps clearly into the light, exposing the foolish, complicated props humankind has created in order to explain the universe.

Although there are many intuitive people, often they cannot distinguish between reason and intuition. Indeed, reason is the problem we face when attempting to strengthen and follow our intuition. We get an intuitive feeling first. Then reason surfaces, creating conflict and competing for our mind's attention. The second thought is usually stronger and clearer than the first, intuitive thought. Intuition is, therefore, usually pushed to the side. Resisting the urge to deny the existence and relevance of intuition can strengthen it. In all situations, make it a habit to hold onto your first intuitive feeling, thereby saving it from being destroyed by reason. Continued practice of this habit will help you to heighten your intuitive ability. Every faculty needs to be nurtured. Develop the self-confidence that will allow you listen to your intuition.

Women are naturally more intuitive than men. This is due to the fact that women are usually more receptive and sympathetic, and therefore are better equipped to perceive and heed their intuition. However, be it in a man or woman, intuition is the faculty of a sympathetic heart that feels deeply. Interestingly, the intuition of cats and dogs is clearer than that of humans. They seem to know when something, an accident or death, is going to occur. Often times, they try to warn their human counterparts, but we are so consumed with our own lives we generally ignore these warnings.

In order to fully embrace your intuition, you must release yourself from the self-imposed resistance that keeps you tethered to this Earth. This resistance is born of desire, need, lack of patience, a self-serving attitude, aggression and greed. These states of being do us no good. They prevent us from entering into the right phase of being—a phase of calm, stillness, tranquility and peace. The phase of right being is required for living Divinely in this world. When we achieve this phase we are able to float freely into the next realm of infinite possibility. It is wonder, innocence, purity, fun, courage, adventure, magic and joy that allow us to rise to new, heavenly heights where all is seen and known.

In order to enter into a space that is beneficial for the full utilization of your intuition, you need to enter into a state of deep relaxation that, in turn, stimulates the pituitary gland. Stimulation of this gland helps activate the qualities detailed in the preceding paragraph and embrace the possibilities attendant with heightened intuition. Relaxation, not concentration or intensity of mind and heart, is the key. Through deep relaxation, we enter into a state of flow. Our "little will" surrenders to the will of God, and we become more aware of the omens and portents that exist all around us. These omens and portents can then be interpreted by the intuitive mind, providing us with the helpful, useful understanding and knowledge.

Training and practice, along with patience and confidence, is crucial to the development of intuition. Remember, the one without intuition has neither direction nor power. He is at the mercy of his own negative patterns and soon suffers the consequences of foolish relationship choices. One can develop intuitive capabilities and intuitive logic by applying the principles and exercises in this book. Intuitive logic is the highest form of intuition and logic. It is direct knowing with one duty, the justification of intuition.

Meditation and Intuition

As we have said, the natural law of intuition requires that the subconscious mind be cleared of all negative patterns. Only then can our intuitive intelligence be our guide. When intuition rules negative patterns from above, they are unable to rule over us and defeat us. Meditation is essential, as meditation clears our emotional conflicts, thereby restoring self-healing and harmony. Through meditation, we create the space for intuition to prevail.

There are many methods of meditation. One method involves the use of sound. Sound effectively cuts through the garbage of the subconscious mind. For this purpose, an efficient and eloquent sound is ONG. ONG is called a seed mantra. All other mantras originate from ONG and return to it. ONG takes you from duality to divinity, from fear to love. It is the creative power.

There is a clear distinction between OM and ONG. OM is God in an unmanifested state, while ONG is the infinite creative energy manifested. OM does not reach the palate when vibrated. ONG, on the other hand, does.

The secret to effectiveness when vibrating ONG is to vibrate at the brow point, or sixth chakra, via the nose. In this way, the sound of ONG pushes the breath from the back of the throat into the nose, creating vibrations in the nasal cavities. When we make the breath nasal, it becomes the breath of life. Negative patterns are neutralized, thus allowing your intuition to become automatic. Moreover, by creating vibrations in the nasal cavities, ONG stimulates the higher glands, by driving the hypothalamus to rotate in rhythm with the pulse of the pituitary gland. This, in turn, causes the glandular system to synchronize with the pulse of the body's magnetic field, thereby sealing all the cavities of the aura.

It is recommended that you use ONG to tune in at the beginning of all spiritual work. This will purify the mental, spiritual and physical bodies, and balance the lunar and solar forces so that you are able to burn karma. *(See the Adi Mantra, page 162)*

Activating your intuition is as simple as breathing. You need only to take time to relax and open your third eye. We all have the right to earn the gift of intuitive sight. And now, more than ever, intuition is needed, for the time of self-teaching is drawing near. Mankind must become more empowered. We must begin to rely on ourselves for information, confirmation and truth. We must acknowledge the light in the darkness, and in so doing, take responsibility for our spiritual actions here on Earth.

Commit to engaging the third eye each morning and evening. By doing this, you will cross barriers, because the moment you relate to the unseen you become energized. Every 72 hours you change. Indeed, motion is the principle of life. It is only God who does not change. Embrace this notion and heed the word of the scripture:

"O man, go and lie flat at the feet of anyone who can show you how to relate to the unseen."

Those who master and vibrate at the sixth chakra are released from problems as duality dissolves and unity is established in the consciousness. It is here that we meditate on our true natures. We speak consciously because we are aware of the far-reaching effects of our words. We completely connect with the internal voice of God called consciousness. We gain psychic powers and destroy all karma we have incurred in past lives. Mastery brings the knowledge that spiritual devotion is the only sure path to liberation.

MANTRA: NEUTRALIZE THE SUBCONSCIOUS MIND

Position:

Sit in easy pose with your legs crossed or in a comfortable meditative position, keeping your spine straight.

Eyes are closed and focused at the point between your brows—the third eye.

The hands are in prayer pose (palm to palm) at the chest. Thumbs touch the sternum.

Mantra: ONG

Simply inhale fully and vibrate ONG on the exhale, pushing the sound out through your nose, until you run out of breath. Repeat 11 times.

OOOHHHHHHNNNNNNNNNGGG

When finished, sit motionless with long, deep breathing while meditating at the third eye.

Comments:

You will notice that mind, body and spirit will soon come into balance as the subconscious starts releasing all its negative patterns.

A CD recording of the mantra ONG can be found on *Triple Mantra* and *OM House*, available through Rootlight, Inc. For order information, please see the back of the book.

God is constant and immutable.
Concentrating on Divinity moves
the relationship from the illusion of
duality to the reality of Oneness.
This is the relationship which can
successfully overcome any challenge
and survive indefinitely.

CHAPTER FOUR

The Head versus the Heart

Let me try to dispel the confusion between the head and heart. The expression *"Follow your heart and you will shine like the Sun"* means *"If you follow your intuition, you will make the choices that make you happiest."* The heart center is the reflection of the Sun in us. It is the seat of the soul and the door to the invisible world. It is a bank of wisdom, since it contains many lifetimes of experiences. It sees the unseen, knows the unknown, feels the unfeelable, and hears the unheard. It knows the past, present and future. The heart cannot be limited in any kind of way; it knows no time or space. It is the God in us, whereas the mind is often limited by the barriers of our five senses of perception. It tends to rely on both our negative patterns and the experiences and conditions of this lifetime.

We have three minds: negative, positive and intuitive. The negative mind computes the possible obstacles of a situation. Our positive mind reveals the opportunities. Our intuitive mind tells us exactly the safest and best course of action for our highest good.

The mind is primarily ruled by the Moon. As a result, we fluctuate between the positive and negative poles of the mind without ever using the intuitive mind. The intuitive mind cannot operate when we are in the loop of fear, doubt and psychological patterns. As long as the mind is in duality, the intuition cannot operate. Intuition is the guidance of the soul. Its seat is in the third eye at the sixth chakra. Since meditation leads to self-awareness, and

ALCHEMY OF LOVE RELATIONSHIPS

self-awareness leads to conscious living, meditation is an essential key that takes you out of the loop of automatic living. When subconscious patterns are neutralized, they cannot overpower a conscious person. As a result, the mind puts itself at the service of the soul.

Since the soul has many lifetimes of experiences, its wisdom is superior to that of the mind, which only relies on the experiences of this present life. It is ruled by the Sun, whereas the head is ruled by the Moon. The one who follows the voice of the soul by connecting with the third eye (the center of intuition) always finds happiness. Those who experience pain and undue struggle are stuck in the duality of the mind, which is clouded by patterns and results in automatic and unconscious living. If you follow the heart, the universe will guide you. If you follow the head, make sure you stay in clear contact with your intuitive mind, otherwise you will fall into the pit of duality and confusion.

A common example of following the head is how we judge people and things by the way they look, not considering that a person can be exceptionally beautiful on the outside and horribly ugly on the inside! Since people are often ruled by their heads, they will enter into relationships with "attractive-on-the-outside" people and end up creating unhealthy relationships repeatedly. The stress of these relationships whittles away the life force, leaving one drained, exhausted, even sleepless. The tension existing within the constraints of such relationships weakens the electromagnetic field and digestive system. It also lowers the regenerative functions of the immune and cardiovascular systems and leaves the body susceptible to all sorts of illnesses and diseases. These destructive love relationships can even attract further adversity!

Those who follow their heads into relationships go for the wrong partners, and as we all know, the wrong mate can drive you nuts! He or she can stress you out, grate on your nerves and choke your life force to death. When you engage in sexual intercourse, you and your partner exchange vital energy, and after union, your partner remains in your aura for years. This stressful, negative presence can prevent the proper flow of energy throughout your psychic body. This is extremely detrimental to your mental, emotional and spiritual health. Those who remain in stressful relationships or compulsively travel from one to another, create sustained and chronic stress. In addition, they tend to develop poor eating and improper breathing habits, due to the constant release of hormones needed to deal with all the tension and stress. Consequently, they contract debilitating conditions such as diabetes and cancer and may even develop blood clots.

To enter a healthy relationship, therefore, one needs to act with the heart supported by the intuitive mind. The proper relationship nurtures, strengthens and revitalizes, makes you joyful, blissful and fulfilled, and it generally improves your health. This is achieved through always living consciously from the heart. When you do this, your perceptions become stronger, your life happier, and you can conquer your old psychic patterns—thus attracting all the right relationships forever after! Furthermore, conscious living imparts intuition and frees you from the karmic influences of the past—the best way to erase karmic influences. Last, but not least, your good actions will be rewarded by the beneficent planet Jupiter.

The aura is mostly unseen
by the naked eye.
It is one of the most powerful
lines of defense we have.
Our aura protects us against visible,
as well as invisible, influences.

CHAPTER FIVE

The Importance of the Aura

Everyone has a unique aura, which vibrates at a particular frequency. Our frequency will not only determine who and what we like or dislike, but also what experiences and people we attract in life.

The Aura: A Brief Overview

What exactly is the aura? The aura, or electromagnetic field, is the light emitted by our essential vitality, or Ojas. It is responsible for fending off disease, and it maintains the integrity of the mind and body. We can consult the aura to locate any energy imbalances that may have developed in a particular individual. Sometimes, the condition of one's aura can be read through the complexion, luster of the eyes and, to a certain extent, the pulse. Its condition is also revealed by the energy and integrity of one's character, and the degree of creativity he possesses.

The aura is a psychic field of energy that surrounds the body. It follows the Law of the Triangle. When the male and female principles are united, they create a third principle. In this case it is an energy field surrounding the body, called the aura. A perfect union will create a strong and beautiful aura that radiates a protective light. Outside forces cannot affect a person with such an aura. When the union is less balanced, it generates a shrinking and dull aura. Negative influences always interfere with a person who has a weak aura.

Everything from the atom to the human has an aura. In the atom, the male and female principles are respectively represented by the proton and electron, whereas in humans they respectively stand for the electric and magnetic forces. The body constantly absorbs and emits energy. The electric part of our aura gives off energy, while the magnetic part attracts and absorbs energy. On one hand, the electric force helps the brain in the carrying of messages. It helps the nerves, arteries, veins and the circulation of blood. On the other hand, the magnetic force makes one attractive. In addition, it rebuilds and rejuvenates the body.

There are also additional forces, such as the divine shield and the arcline, that surround the physical body but go unseen by most eyes. There must be damage to the divine shield before one dies. Such damage is induced by negativity generated by the untempered passions of the three lower chakras. The strength of the arcline will determine how lucky you are.

Humans constantly interact aurically with minerals, trees, animals and other humans. After living in a house or especially sleeping in a room for some time, the space becomes magnetized by one's auric fluid. Similarly, every object we touch or the clothes and jewelry we wear receive the imprint of our auric energy. That is the reason why trained mystics can hold a ring, for example, of someone unknown and by concentration, can tell you about the owner. This is called psychometry. Mystics do this via the imprint of the auric energy left by the owner of that ring.

Among the auric imprints left on objects, dwellings or people, intimate contact creates deeper ones. Intimate or sexual contact leaves a very strong imprint upon those involved. These imprints are very difficult to remove. If a woman engages in sexual intercourse with twenty men, those men will show in her aura. The same is true for a man. Each imprint takes at least three years to clear.

Everything in this world happens according to time and space. We cannot stop time, but we can change space in order to positively affect our destiny. The strength or weakness of our psycho-electromagnetic field will determine the space of our human experience. A weak aura can put you at the wrong place and time and completely destroy your whole life. When the electromagnetic field, or aura, is strong it puts us in the right place at the right time, so that we may be fulfilled and happy. When the aura is strong we deflect all forms of abuse and adversity. A strong aura also keeps us healthy and energetic, and most importantly, we attract the right partner. The aura can be strengthened by meditation, proper diet and breathing habits, positive thinking, yoga, exercise, and most of all, conscious living.

Ninety percent of the human is unseen, and only 10 percent is seen. The tragedy is that men and women rely 90 percent of the time on the 10 percent they see and 10 percent of the time on the 90 percent they do not see. The fact is that the forces that direct our lives are mostly unseen. This holds true for the aura. The aura, which is mostly unseen by the naked eye, is one of the most powerful lines of defense we have. Our aura protects us against visible as well as invisible influences. We take care of our bodies by washing and grooming them every day because we can see them. If a person stops showering for two weeks, he/she will begin to stink and people will smell him/her at a distance. The aura is the most powerful protection we have against adversity, yet we do not take care of it the way we do the physical body. The aura is of vital importance because it can protect the physical body. When the electromagnetic field is weak, we experience verbal, physical, emotional, mental, sexual and/or financial abuse. We attract diseases and are prone to accidents and calamities. We experience poverty and hardship. Furthermore, we attract the wrong love partner.

WHAT EXACTLY WEAKENS THE AURA?

The aura is weakened by *functional* and *radical* reasons. The functional reasons are: consumption of alcohol, drugs, tobacco, etc. Not only do these substances weaken the aura, they also cloud our intuition and reduce our ability to be conscious. Remember, do not engage in sexual relations with someone for the first time after you have taken one or more of the above, because you are in a vulnerable space and therefore you will most likely get hurt. Other functional reasons are: poor eating habits, stress, lack of adequate rest, negative thinking, and lack of yoga or physical exercise.

The *radical* reason for a weakened aura is automatic or unconscious living. An example of this is being governed by impulses. It makes you vulnerable to disease and adversity.

If you strengthen your aura by meditation and exercise and continue to live unconsciously, it is exactly like taking aspirin to relieve a headache and hitting your head against a wall. No matter how many meditations you do to strengthen your aura, automatic living will progressively weaken it and make you vulnerable to negativity and adversity. Therefore, the key to maintaining a strong aura is in knowing a consequence before you start a sequence. It is called conscious living or awareness. It is vital to get into a sexual relationship with full awareness.

THE COMPROMISED AURA

Certain factors contribute to the weakening of one's aura. These include the use of pharmaceuticals, dependence on machines and extended hospital stays. In addition, because the aura represents our consciousness, excess stimulation or dissipation resulting from sensory overload, practices such as channeling, exposure to environmental pollutants, excessive sexual behavior and overexposure to mass media can prove detrimental. Indeed, our aura is damaged whenever we give our minds over to external influences and personalities.

Most of us find ourselves in wrong relationships because our aura has been compromised.

What causes us to engage in behaviors and thought patterns that weaken our aura? The first cause, low self-esteem, is internal. The second cause, the energy we draw from outside sources, is external. The third cause lies with the thoughts and feelings of our mind.

Low self-esteem can be initiated immediately. Indeed, it can occur at the very moment of conception. When a child's parents are not together in a mental projectile, angular energy beam, and/or they do not have mental harmony, the very act of conception can cause the child that is born to them to have low self-esteem. The ninth month of pregnancy is also a critical time in terms of forming the building blocks of self-esteem. If either the mother or father is beset by intense depression, their condition may manifest as low self-esteem in their child. Household difficulties, social problems, biological troubles, sociological handicaps and psychological mis-management also have a negative impact on the child during the ninth month of pregnancy.

The environment a child is born into is equally important. When a child is raised in an environment of unscientific love, he is deprived of the inner seeding of the personality. All environmental inner centers can then be stretched into diagonal forms, damaging the triangles of the reserve and projective energies. When our self-esteem and aura are damaged in childhood, we generally carry that damage with us into adulthood.

As we move from childhood into adulthood, however, we become responsible for the upkeep of our auras. The energy we draw from outside sources is critical to the maintenance of a healthy aura. This energy is mainly derived from food and breath. An improper diet denies our bodies of the restorative energy of nutrients. This, in turn, weakens our ability to maintain a strong energy field and remain in perfect health. Shallow or hurried respiration also impacts our aura in a negative manner.

In addition to our choices with regard to the food we eat and the manner in which we breathe, the state of our mind is an important factor in building a bright, beautiful aura. We must resist all mental distractions including pettiness, gossip, worry and/or excessive focus as such distractions dissipate our mental energy.

REVITALIZING YOUR AURA

It is important to state, from the onset, that all action taken to improve your aura must be detached from the ordinary motivations of personal achievement and/or acquisition. Having said that, we can now continue with an explanation of how you can strengthen your aura.

The aura is essentially a manifestation of our daily thoughts and actions. Therefore, adopting a positive mental attitude and healthy lifestyle can help it flourish. Pranayama, gems, mantra and meditation are all tools we can employ to strengthen and brighten our aura. Create your own sacred space by devoting a room in your home to meditation or creating an altar. Such a space will serve to help connect you with your cosmic being, or inner self.

When you have achieved a balance between the tattvas and the chakras, your personality becomes harmonious, and engaging in dysfunctional behavior is no longer an appealing option. You will have ample reserves through the squares of your being, because energy will flow through your body along proper channels. It is even possible that extra energy will be stored in the energy squares of the body. This extra energy has many beneficial uses. It can help you cope during times of stress, write off the pain of childhood, overcome negative influences, thoughts and people, cope with the inevitable pains and pressures of adulthood, and withstand the projective animosity of social, economic and personal environments.

Life is graceful and healthy when our energies flow freely. By following a spiritual discipline, we can harmonize our nature, and provide Divine grace with material with which to work. We must actively participate, however, by working with the external and internal aspects of our nature. Again, proper diet, right thinking and meditative practices go a long way in helping the inner depth of our being to emerge.

MAINTAIN THE STRENGTH OF YOUR AURA

First, *conscious living* is the best auric protection one has. Always consult the consequence of a sequence before you act. Avoid substances that may cloud your judgment or weaken your aura, such as drugs, alcohol, tobacco, etc.

Second, anyone who wants a strong aura needs to *avoid negativity*, because it pollutes the blood and weakens the electromagnetic field. Don't project negativity about yourself or others.

Third, *uplifting others* will attract the grace of God in your life.

Fourth, the *power of sound* through chanting mantras along with *proper breathing* will protect and strengthen the aura.

THE AURA AND SOUND

There are two main forms of intercourse. The first is sexual intercourse which you need a partner to perform. The second form is the only type you can do alone. It is called *divine intercourse*. This form of intercourse will wipe out any weakness in your destiny. It will harmonize your individual aura with the universe, so that your genuine desires may be fulfilled. It will give you intuitive intelligence, so that you may know whether you are going in the right direction or not.

Divine intercourse is the art of creating sound currents. It is called *Naad (Na-had') yoga*. Naad yoga will invoke the creative energy which runs between you and the universe. Naad is the science of using mantras. A mantra is a mental vibratory projection based on a particular sound used to regulate the mind.

Sound is the blueprint of creation. God spoke and created the space in which creation took place. Everything comes from sound and returns to sound.

The most powerful instrument one has is the voice. One can create the divine heat of love and penetrate the mind, body and soul with sound. Sound can completely rearrange the molecular structure of the brain and cells, as well as raise one's electromagnetic frequency. In addition, sound can synchronize right and left brain hemispheres and totally affect the brain waves. In fact, anyone who knows how to use sound can effect positive changes in both his/her body and surroundings.

How does one come to such an elevated state of awareness? This is easily achieved through control of the limbic system. The limbic system (primary brain) sits on top of the spine. This part of the brain controls the primal aspect of the personality, which is responsible for impulsive and instinctive behavior. The one who is at the mercy of impulsive behavior often makes fatal mistakes. Control of the limbic system automatically bestows a meditative mind. A meditative mind stops impulsive behavior, centers your energy and brings feelings of peace and well-being. From that point, wise decisions can be reached in the choice of a partner.

Certain sounds can be used to affect the limbic system and control the frontal lobe. Controlling the frontal lobe automatically lends control of the personality. There are reflex points all around the mouth, but above all, there are 84 energy points inside the palate. The hypothalamus sits on the palate. When you chant or vibrate a mantra, the tongue, which represents the male organ, or Sun, goes in intercourse with the upper palate, which stands for the Moon. As a result, the hypothalamus is stimulated, and in exchange, the pituitary and pineal glands are also stimulated. These glands regulate the autonomic nervous system, which in turn protects us from negativity. Through this process, the neuron patterns in the brain are realigned with the past, present and future. Once this is achieved, the molecular frequency of the brain changes, thereby affecting the whole molecular structure of the body. As a result, one receives the blessing of intuitive intelligence. The most direct way to move from duality to Divinity is through sound. Duality will make you confused and helpless with your constant fluctuations, whereas Divinity will bring you the true satisfaction that comes with your heart's genuine desires.

There are two sounds you can use to strengthen your aura: ONG *(Chapter 3, page 29)* and RAMA.

MANTRA: STRENGTHEN THE AURA

There are two principles in each of us. They are the father (male) principle and the mother (female) principle. They stand for the electric and magnetic force respectively. Their corresponding sounds are RA and MA.

RA and MA are two sounds which fortify and harmonize the electric and magnetic forces. When RA and MA are chanted together, they create a strong and protective aura.

Position:
Sit in a comfortable position, either with the legs crossed or the feet flat on the floor. Spine is erect. Eyes are closed and focused at the third eye point between the brows.

Mantra: RA-MA
Inhale slowly and deeply through the nose. Hold for a few seconds and chant on the exhale:

RRRAAAAAAAAA-MMMAAAAAAAAA

Repetitions:
11 times is sufficient to strengthen your aura.

The heart cannot be limited in any
kind of way; it knows no time or space.
It is the God in us, whereas the mind is often
limited by the barriers of our five senses
of perception. It tends to rely on both our
negative patterns and the experiences
and conditions of this lifetime.

CHAPTER SIX

Exchange of Vital Fluids:
The Aura and Sex

The aura plays a significant role in any love relationship. When a man and woman engage sexually, there is an automatic exchange of vital fluids. This exchange is recorded in their respective auras. When you have sex with someone, he or she shows in your aura for at least three years. Incidentally, most trained mystics on the path of Light can see this imprint in your energy field.

It is extremely important, then, that you be fully aware when you open your energy field to another. When you begin to get intimately involved with someone, do so within the boundaries of a protective aura and keen, self-protective intuition. The bonding must be right. Do not have sex just to check someone out. Many have experienced wonderful platonic relationships with the opposite sex. Engaging in sex alters the platonic nature of the relationship, however, and the friendship suffers because you are now in each other's auras. What was once a wonderful relationship often becomes unpleasant. Your friend now seems like a different person.

Just because a platonic relationship is wonderful does not necessarily mean that it will translate into a productive love relationship. Indeed, many platonic relationships are best left platonic. Don't spoil your friendships with a lack of awareness and sexual curiosity. How do you know when to keep a relationship platonic and when to transform it into a love relationship? Remember to engage in a

45

love relationship with 100 percent awareness, guided by your intuition.

Sex without love depletes one's vitality and deranges the emotions. Sexual contact with many partners transfers the toxins that are secreted. These toxins can circumvent a person's immune system and lodge in the deep tissues. Moreover, when we have several sexual partners, these partners show up in our electromagnetic field creating a clouded aura whose light has faded. People with multiple partners always look older than they actually are. If you have sex with such a person, one with a weakened immune system and shrunken aura, you too will be depleted of your vitality.

Women are especially sensitive to the blending of auras, as the imprint of the male on the female is intense. When a woman jumps from one partner to the next, blending her aura here and there, her aura weakens and her true identity is lost. She feels the weight of guilt and shame. She is weakened emotionally.

The mental frequency and auric strength of the woman are crucial in determining the potency, or impotency, of her mate. When a woman's aura is expanded to seven feet, it energizes her partner after intercourse, rather than depleting him. Remember, women are sixteen times stronger, more intelligent and more sacred than men. A woman should never have sex with her partner once she has mixed her aura with a second man. Her first partner will suffer an auric injury that penetrates his behavior and temperament, causing him to go insane. Men, while they do not experience the same negative effects detailed in the preceding paragraph, are very delicate in this way. Indeed, the very sensitive male can even experience an auric shock when the indiscretion of his partner has been in thought rather than deed. This reality explains why some men are more potent than others when it comes to women. The man who has suffered multiple experiences of auric shock is rendered incapable of attracting and maintaining a woman. A woman, then, must be particularly careful in her choice of a mate. Moreover, she must encourage her partner to maintain his health.

Regarding Married Couples and Committed Partners

After repeated sexual intercourse and exchange of vital fluids, a third, invisible entity is created on the astral plane. This invisible astral entity is created from the energy of the two partners. It is fully alive. So, in actuality, there are three aspects to any long-standing love relationship: the two people as individuals, the two people as a couple, and the third entity they create together.

When a couple separates, they often experience a heart-wrenching pain. This pain will last as long as it takes for the astral entity they have created to disintegrate. Although the physical parting may take as little as a day, the disintegration of the invisible entity takes at least three years. During this time, the partners will go through mental and emotional turmoil. This is also the case in situations where one of the two partners has died. Interestingly, in instances where the couple has been together for a long time, for example a couple of advanced age, the astral entity is extremely strong. This accounts for why, when one partner dies or becomes ill, the other may also die or become ill.

A Final Note

Conscious living will bring happiness, even if this is not the intended goal. By mastering the second chakra, the yogi becomes a beloved figure. He radiates like the sun, freeing himself from enemies and commanding the love of all animals and people. The elements come under his domain. With his lustful desires conquered, the yogi's creative energy is redirected and he becomes well versed in the arts of poetry, prose and reasoned discourse.

Interestingly, the normal span of potency for a yogi or kabbalist is equal to the span of his life, while potency in the United States generally wanes in one's late 30s or early 40s.

Always keep in mind that sexual freedom does not mean sexual exploitation. It means sexual preservation, reverence and choice. When there is love and respect between two people both partners are strengthened. The woman feels creative, vital, expansive and secure. The man feels uplifted, cared for, confident and potent.

MEDITATION: OVERCOME NEGATIVE PATTERNS

GANPATI KRIYA

This meditation will help you deal with your negative patterns. Ganpati Kriya (pronounced gun-puti) is a very sacred kriya. It is called the impossible-possible kriya, where all negativity from the past and present will be redeemed. Ganpati is sometimes called Mangalam, the God of Happiness. This meditation deals with samskaras, karma, and dharam. It will take away all samskaras, all the negative karmas you carry from past lives and have to pay for now. The suffering or happiness we currently experience is due to past debt or past credit. It also takes away the karma you create from what you do in your daily life. It creates the way for dharam—what good you do today will be rewarded tomorrow.

Pressing the thumb to each finger tip applies the science through which one can rewrite his or her destiny. It balances the five elements, thereby bringing the mind, body, emotions and spirit into harmony. This is Ganpati Kriya.

Position:
Sit in an easy pose, spine straight, elbows straight, wrists resting on knees. You will be pressing your thumb to each finger alternatively with each sound. Keep the eyes closed.

Mantra:
Chant in an even rhythm to this simple tune:

SA TA NA MA RA MA DA SA SA SAY SO HUNG

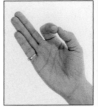 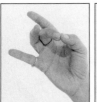  

SA	Thumb to the index finger. (Jupiter/Water)	*Birth*
TA	Thumb to the middle finger. (Saturn/Fire)	*Existence*
NA	Thumb to the ring finger. (Sun/Air)	*Death*
MA	Thumb to the baby finger. (Mercury/Ether)	*Rebirth*
RA	Thumb to the index finger.	*Sun*
MA	Thumb to the middle finger	*Moon*
DA	Thumb to the ring finger.	*Earth*
SA	Thumb to the baby finger.	*Infinity*
SA	Thumb to the index finger.	*Infinity*
SAY	Thumb to the middle finger	*Thou*
SO	Thumb to the ring finger.	*I Am*
HUNG	Thumb to the baby finger.	*Thou*

Time:

Continue for 11 minutes. To end the meditation, inhale deeply, then move and rotate the body as if going through physical spasms. Every muscle must be stretched, squeezed and moved—from the muscles in your face, head and neck, down to your toes. The idea is to circulate the prana to every part of your body. The breath is held for approximately 35 seconds. (Repeat this procedure four times, with the breath held in.) Final step: Inhale, sit calmly, and concentrate on the tip of your nose for 20 seconds. RELAX.

A CD recording of this mantra may be obtained through Rootlight, Inc. Please see the back of the book for details.

Sexual energy is the primary energy of the body and mind, as the sexual fluid produced by both men and women contains a high concentration of minerals and elements crucial to effective nerve balance and brain function. Sexual experience, when performed in the correct consciousness can give one the experience of God and bliss.

CHAPTER SEVEN

The Second Chakra

The second chakra relates to procreation and creativity. Its element is water. Its color is either luminous white or light blue. The sense of taste is dominant.

The second chakra is located in the area of the sex organs and rules the realm sexuality and vitality. On a physical level, the second chakra is associated with excretion and reproduction. On a spiritual level, it is the seat of the individual and collective unconscious. It is the storehouse of all samskaras, the past mental impressions stored in the form of archetypes.

The physical manifestations of the water element, known as apastattwa, are the kidneys, sex glands and lymphatic system. They can be grouped together under the term *varuna-granthi*. People with a predominance of varuna-granthi tend to be amiable, displaying a pleasing and charming manner. When you vibrate at the second chakra, you tend to sleep between eight and ten hours per night in the fetal position.

The second chakra, as the center of our most primitive and deep-rooted instincts, is associated with pleasure seeking via the tongue and genital organs. The emphasis here is on enjoyment and the sensations that accompany food, drink and sexual interaction. When this chakra is activated, its energies may manifest as an overwhelming desire or craving for corporeal satisfactions. Second chakra difficulties result from the energy loss that occurs when we over-indulge and/or

---

The Second Chakra
CENTER OF SEXUALITY AND FAMILY

Planet: Mars

Metal: Iron

Angel: Kamael

Negative Qualities: over-sexed, compulsive sexuality

Positive Qualities: creativity, idealism, philosophical with the ability to contribute new ideas.

Effects: When the second chakra is not functioning properly, everything becomes sexual. The reality is, in its entirety, a sensual and sexual state. Because the person is not in line with higher consciousness, the mind, body and soul suffer from troubles.

Communication: Sexually laced, aggressive and abusive

Consciousness: Sex maniac and sadist who enjoys inflicting pain during sex.

Work Organ: Sex Organ

Vayu (Air): Apana Vayu, the air that expels the semen from the male organ; urine for both sexes; and that which pushes the child from the womb during birth.

---

corrupt sensory pleasures. As the center of our most primitive and deep-rooted instincts, purification of the second chakra allows us to transcend our animal nature.

The second chakra also contains positive power. It rules the astral plane, where fantasy and joy reside. Moreover the sensuality found therein is the force that, when channeled properly, drives creative and artistic expression.

The Second Chakra and Sexuality

Sexuality and sensuality are important components of a romantic relationship. Indeed, at its purest level, a sexual relationship involves the interlocking of higher consciousness. It regenerates the body and psyche of both individuals. One gains the energy and confidence to take the initiative that spawns success. The sixth sense is activated and intuition is heightened. In order to reap the benefits of such a relationship, however, it must be regarded as sacred and approached with reverence. In this way sex becomes a healthy addition to the union, rather than a disruptive act that causes disharmony to both the partners and the partnership.

A sexual relationship governed solely by the second chakra is one in which sexuality and sensuality serve as the primary focus. Such a relationship does not include reverence. As a result, jealousy and envy enter and take root. The relationship comes to be ruled by insecurity and an unenlightened desire for the mere exchange of emotions and physicality. With an exclusion of the divine, the relationship disintegrates into a painful tragedy that weakens both partners. It is important to keep in mind, then, that sex should neither be used as the glue that holds a relationship together, or the acid that eats it away, nor should sex be employed as a weapon for vengeance or character assassination.

THE SEXUAL GLANDS

The sexual glands, or gonads, of the female are the ovaries. They begin to function at puberty, producing the hormones responsible for secondary sexual characteristics such as the development of sex organs, the female form and body hair. In addition to hormones, the ovaries excrete an ovum every twenty-eight days.

The male sexual gonads are the testes. Like the ovaries, the testes are responsible for secondary sexual characteristics such as change in voice, hair growth, and muscular development. In addition to hormones, the testes excrete sperm cells.

The gonads are the glands of creation. This creative energy may be used on either the physical or mental plane. There is little doubt, however, that the hormones secreted by these glands form the foundation for our mental, emotional and physical health. Therefore, their normal functioning and cooperation with the other glands in the endocrine system is essential.

SEX AND THE YOUNG

Sexuality on the physical plane is intercourse. On the higher plane, it is pure creativity. The yogic scriptures provide both men and women with guidelines for the development of healthy, positive, nurturing sexuality. They state that a man should not engage in sexual intercourse until his early 20's due to the fact that his sex organs have yet to mature fully. Before that time, a man's semen—the essential oil of his body—is thin and his bone marrow has not developed to the point where it can properly sustain his bone structure. The energy and strength he exerts as he grows cannot be compensated for by diet and exercise alone. The elementary energy of the sperm is needed. Moreover, premature sexual discharge inhibits the cells of the brain and neurological system. Premature sexual relations can have a detrimental impact on an emotional level as well. If a man has sex before he is emotionally and physically ready for it, his chances of impotency increase. Indeed, during mid-life, he may very well experience periodic episodes or complete impotency.

The female sexual organs are not developed until the age of 17. Under no circumstances should a woman engage, either emotionally or physically, in sexual activity before she reaches 17. Difficulties with bone density and calcium can manifest later in life for women who participate in sex at too young an age.

Yin (female) and yang (male) energies do not blend properly for the young couple. The nervous system comes under tremendous strain, and negativity is established. This is especially true for women. Therefore, women who engage in sexual relations at an early age are at risk for developing problems with the nerves and temperament. Should this occur, vitamins, yoga and exercise are indicated for nervous issues, while meditation is indicated for temperamental difficulties.

SEX AND THE MATURE COUPLE

Sex is a sensory experience, centered in the pituitary gland, whose purpose is to create an interlocking vibration between a man and a woman. The olfactory sense is primary to sexual intercourse, because when the pituitary gland is triggered by smell it orders the central nervous system to prepare the individual for sexual contact. Moreover, while sexual intercourse is performed at the second chakra, it is initiated at the sixth. The sixth chakra is the center of creativity and command. It commissions every human activity and works through fragrance.

Too much, or too little, sex impacts negatively on the glandular system. Stimulated during the act of intercourse, glandular activity must accelerate to an optimum level to allow for complete relaxation.

Before intercourse, both partners should clean themselves in order to maintain proper hygiene. Water is a powerful agent of purification for the body and mind. The woman should bathe and douche to rid herself of any odors. This process of cleansing is not only conducive to proper hygiene, it also acts to affirm her sacredness. For sanitary reasons and the health of his partner, the man should wash his sexual organ.

Well-functioning intestines are required for a strong energy field and healthy intimate interaction. Indications of unhealthy intestines include constipation, halitosis, flatulence, skin disturbances and vaginal infections. During intercourse, the lower colon and rectum should be empty; otherwise the woman may experience vaginal discomfort and become vulnerable to infections. Moreover, if the lower colon and rectum are not clear, the movement of the penis could cause the stool to backtrack and damage the iliocaecal valve.

The physical, emotional and mental strength of a man is reflected in his semen. There are 80 drops of semen per ejaculation and 80 drops of blood per semen. A man's semen feeds his nerves. When the semen is in short supply, the nerves are weakened. Therefore, it is highly advisable to be in peak physical condition before engaging in sexual intercourse. Moreover, the sympathetic, parasympathetic and central nervous systems must be in perfect balance in order for intercourse to benefit the couple. If the sympathetic nervous system is out of balance, the man may experience premature ejaculation. If the parasympathetic nervous system is out of balance, he may be unable to achieve an erection. And finally, if the central nervous system is not in proper working order, he may be unable to ejaculate. In order to avoid a weakening of the nervous system, it is necessary that a man preserve his seed. To remain potent he should also massage the area between his penis and anus after urination.

MASTURBATION AND WET DREAMS

Masturbation and wet dreams are a part of physical life. It is important to know their impact on the human system.

Men who masturbate on a regular basis negatively impact their pituitary gland. This negative impact manifests as a diminished ability to concentrate and a wasting of energy. When a man masturbates, he is deprived of the emotional and energetic exchange that occurs between two partners. This exchange helps to maintain a balanced system. Without it, a man's vata is aggravated, leaving him vulnerable to disease. Masturbation also over-stimulates the imagination, making one vulnerable to the destructive forces of the lower astral worlds and open to negative psychic or astral forces.

Women do not experience the same ill effects that men do in regard to self-stimulation. Women, however, should take care to strengthen themselves by creating a bright auric body through meditation, yoga and healthy living.

One wet dream is the equivalent of seven instances of sexual intercourse. It exerts tremendous pressure on the nervous system and the mind. After a wet dream, one should drink warm water mixed with lemon juice.

SEX AND HEALTH

Most of us have been taught to view sex in terms of pleasure and reproduction. We have not, however, been educated as to the need for sexual moderation. Sexual energy is the primary energy of the body and mind, as the sexual fluid produced by both men and women contains a high concentration of minerals and elements crucial for effective nerve balance and brain function. When the sexual fluid is allowed to mature, it is reabsorbed into the body, and its essence, or Ojas, is transported to the spinal fluid. When used properly, sexual energy keeps the body vital, strengthens the nerves and lends extreme zeal to all receptive and projective organs. Sexual experience, when performed in the correct consciousness, can also give one the experience of God and bliss. This experience is only possible, however, when your sexual batteries are charged and you are in possession of real potency.

If sexual energy is misused or overused, and the mind is not trained to control it, a general weakness of character will be present along with duality in the personality and cowardice in behavior. Mental disturbance and dullness are often heightened, with a concurrent reduction of mental clarity. Running your mind without Ojas is like running a car without oil. You will quickly wear out. Life is filled with pain, unhappiness and instability. Our modern day lifestyle of easy divorce, frequent sexual partners, broken families and a psychological inability to form right relationships attests to the fact that many of us are not using our sexual energy wisely.

Ojas, which means vigor, is the subtle, essential essence of the immune and reproductive systems, all vital secretions and the heat in our tissues. It is a key component of sexual energy. Located in the heart center, Ojas—the sap of our essential life energy—issues forth giving the body stability and support. However, know that Ojas is not a physical substance. When our level of Ojas is sufficient, we are healthy. When it is deficient, we experience disease. Indeed, health problems will come to us in the parts of the body where the level of Ojas is low. Similarly, when the Ojas is completely destroyed, death enters. When it is sustained, life endures. Our levels of Ojas decrease with anger, hunger, worry, sorrow, excessive work, and inappropriate use of sexual energy.

Traditional Chinese medicine holds that the heart is directly affected by anxiety and/or intense emotions, such as excessive joy, passion and greed, which cause us to make poor decisions and lifestyle choices. (Abuses of sexual energy generally involve intense emotion.) When these emotions are not anchored in pure balance, they are detrimental to the Ojas, as they burn yin. (Yin is the water-like substance of our flesh.) Yin deficiency produces symptoms such as a drop in hormone levels, fatigue, dry skin, thin bones and weakened immunity. Moreover, Dr. Zhu Dan Xi, the leader of one of the four great schools of Chinese medical thought, maintained that the root of all disease is "heart fire." This was the term applied to the burning pursuit of desires that creates the excess heart heat that consumes yin. According to traditional Chinese medical thought, Universal Energy obtained through meditative practices is the only source of yin replenishment.

Approximately 90% of your sexual energy is used to repair and rejuvenate the organs of the body. Most physical diseases, then, are related to a wrong use of sexual energy. Sexual indulgence causes Vata (air) or Pitta (fire) disorders as it depletes water (the reproductive fluid), which is the strongest energy our body has to help keep it in check. One becomes more susceptible to infectious diseases. As we have said, excessive sexual activity and/or an inappropriate use of sexual energy decrease Ojas, the essential energy of our immune system. A low level of Ojas leads to chronic, degenerative diseases and premature aging, as well as nervous disorders and hard to treat infections. (AIDS is an example of an Ojas disease.) If you find that you have a low level of Ojas, you can help to replenish it with milk, ghee and tonic herbs. Meditation practices and, of course, sexual moderation are also indicated. Furthermore, one is encouraged to rid the body of toxins, as a body free of toxins contributes to a mild sex drive that is easy to satisfy.

The existence of a diminished sex drive also needs to be addressed. Sexual debility can be caused by many factors such as negative emotions, a low level of energy that comes from over-work, excessive exercise, stress, trauma, extra body weight or too little body weight, weak kidneys and a lack of confidence. For men, especially, confidence is essential to a healthy sex drive. Along with a decreased sex drive, nervousness, palpitations, nocturnal emissions and instances of premature ejaculation can occur.

Our sexually-oriented culture is suspicious of any weakening of the sexual drive. While a diminished sex drive can be an indication of systemic or lifestyle problems, it can also be an indication of the development of higher consciousness and, therefore, good health. Constant preoccupation with sex is unnecessary, because the misuse of it is not for the highest human good. Over-attachment to that which is a worldly comfort leads to mental heaviness. While sex has its distinct place in nature, people often use it as a substitute for other things, particularly creative living. Yogic practice emphasizes control of one's creative energy through a transmutation of the sexual force. This is one of the main ingredients for spiritual development. One is encouraged to transmute the subtle energies of the mind that awaken when the second chakra is stimulated. In this way, sexual energy will promote good health and creativity. When the soul begins to actively function, it assumes control, like the governor of an engine, over the faculties of a human to such an extent that all his energies are disposed to the most completely equilibrated and balanced efforts and usages, and all questions regarding sex conditions come under its dominance. The truly spiritual man or woman whose soul is in active control of the vehicular functions, can no more become a sex maniac or sadist, than he could become a drunkard or a gambler, and he does not need special prohibitive injunctions to dissuade him from engaging in these.

ABSTINENCE

The desire to abstain from sex naturally occurs during acute conditions such as fevers and after childbirth. When we are combating disease or recovering, our interest in sex lowers so that the body can preserve its vitality. Indeed, abstinence from sex is important in the treatment of many health imbalances. For example, when debility, malnourishment and/or convalescence are present, abstinence is a key part of tonification therapy. Abstinence is also valuable when treating mental and nervous disorders, as the sexual fluid lubricates and nourishes the nerve tissues.

Conversely, when abstinence is practiced in an uninformed manner it can become a causative factor in disease. If sexual energy is merely repressed, vitality can stagnate and weaken. Sexual abstinence requires some form of yoga and meditation so that one's sexual energy is transformed into a positive force.

SEX AND ATTRACTION

Men are attracted to the spirit of a woman, not her flesh. When a woman adopts a strong spiritual discipline, her spirit gleams, creating an irresistible allure. Her presence serves to uplift her partner. On the other hand, when a woman is only the substance of her flesh, she is liable to deplete her mate's energy. In order for a woman to help her mate preserve his energy, she must maintain a strong auric body by adopting healthy eating habits, taking the time to care for herself emotionally and physically, and practicing the art of yoga and meditation. Women are men's only hope. Sexual energy can become creative energy for both partners and help facilitate mental and spiritual work when the woman attends to her aura.

It is important to note that when a man uses a woman for her flesh, he degrades himself as well as his partner. The auras of both people collapse, shrinking to less than three feet and opening them to all manner of bad luck, unhappiness, pain and disease.

Remember that sex is a sacred union meant to unite the yin and yang energies. Since a man is born of a woman, it is imperative that he respects women and reveres their sacredness. This will serve to generate peace on Earth. The female principle, or Adi Shakti, is particularly exalted and should be honored. A man's attitude toward women is a direct reflection of his attitude toward life. When a man views his partner as an embodiment of the supreme Shakti, the creative Goddess, she will respond with Bhakti, pure faith and devotion. She will become his high priestess.

CHAPTER EIGHT

Magnifying Your Radiance with Sound Current

As mentioned in the introduction, the main causes of challenges that arise in relationships are deep-rooted subconscious patterns. How do we tear down the unhealthy walls we construct around ourselves? How do we open our hearts to a more complete and fulfilling love relationship? The only way to release the burgeoning fear, doubt, and insecurity that plagues the human condition is to develop a relationship with our expanded identity. The way to conquer destructive patterns—the only way—is with our spirit. Through spirit, we can access our vastness and experience it with comfort. This can be achieved through the power of words or sounds. This primal expression evolves into a true unity with spirit. Sound helps our consciousness expand and facilitate awakening on a spiritual level. Sound raises your frequency and magnifies your radiance, so that you may attract the right partner. Every sound uttered, every noise from us is part of our life force. We can utilize this force and open ourselves to truth and light, thereby expanding our experience of Self and life.

The origin and source of all things, the only true power, is the Logos or the word. *"In the beginning was the word, the word was with God and the word was God."* God is bound by the word, and the word is sound. The saying "I give you my word" comes from the idea that the word and God were synonymous and therefore honored.

Sound keeps the universe in balance. Without it, the whole universe would fall apart and disappear. It is by sound, in sound, and through sound that all things seen and unseen, have been created. Sound is not only the mother of Light, but it also creates life. As a matter of fact, every human being creates a sound to be alive. This can be observed in the continuous sound created by both the breath and the beat of the heart. From birth to death, the continuous cycle is one of sounds.

To penetrate the mysteries of creation, you must master the sound current. By mastering the sound that is your own, you can harness the wisdom of the past, present and future. Sound directs and redirects energy for your safety. It is the healing technology for this age and beyond. It is the God-given elixir that is under-used. It permits our command center, the brain, to maintain its equilibrium under stress. It balances the brain and nervous system. When mastered, it can bring peace where there is panic and fear, and rationality where there is internal chaos.

Ida and *pingala* are the subtle nerves, which respectively correspond to the left and right nostrils. These subtle nerves intertwine around the spine. Our divine force lies in the pillar of equilibrium, referred to as *shushmana* or the central nervous system. To create sound, the human current—*ida* (negative) and *pingala* (positive)—must project a neutral current through the central nervous system, or *shushmana*. The repetition of this sound creates a mantra, which is a mental projection or mind wave. The word "man" means mind and "tra" means trang, which is the wave or the root of an instrument. A mantra is a sound with name and form in it. Repeating sacred words of power or mantra becomes a *sutra* or sound current. Sutra is the pathway to the goal. By repetition of sound you empower yourself to go beyond the ordinary and step into your spirit. Think of it like the sound of the ocean, that eternal licking upon the shore. It is mesmerizing and clear, giving you access to your spirit.

Mantra is a love that flows, a divine shield that protects us like a spiritual immune system. It is a link between you and the divine. Through the mantra meditation, one can receive all powers of creation. Those who perfect their mantras can achieve supreme power, because their mind and neutral self become the same. It's like breaking down the physical confines and allowing sound and spirit to meld and become one. Listening to or chanting mantras is the principle science applied to the art of cleansing the subconscious mind. Mantras are sound currents or words of power used to influence the mind, body and spirit. Through listening or chanting mantras, you can move from darkness to light, from negativity to positivity, from duality to divinity.

The more one chants, the greater its effect. The neutralizing force of the mantra allows the consciousness to become free from limitations of life in the physical world. Those who chant or listen to mantras are relieved from all worries, anxiety, sorrow, fear and disease, and the soul is liberated from the bondage of the senses and the physical body. The soul of the listener merges with the rhythm of the universe. It rises beyond time and space, thereby generating a deep sense of calm. Thus, when a divine bliss fills our hearts, our mind is purified from negativity and fear, and our body from all impurities. Through the clear mind, we see the shining light of the soul; from the light of the soul, we realize the indescribable wisdom of God within the beauty of heaven and earth. Above all, a connection is established with the unseen world, and effortlessly we begin to receive guidance, inspiration, impressions and revelations.

Often, we forget that we already embody a male and female energy within ourselves, that we secrete male and female hormones. Although on the physical level of our reproductive organs, whether we are male or female, each human being possesses only one principle. The split in our creative power makes us feel incomplete and powerless. As a result, we long for a soul mate to complete that union. Therefore, many times we are drawn into relationships in order to feel complete. Perhaps, from our own insecurities we are compelled to look for the other principle in a person of the opposite sex in order to manifest our wholeness. In other words, by birthright, we are whole on the divine and spiritual levels, even though the split in the physical plane drives us toward another human being to feel complete. Our masculine and feminine principles are respectively symbolized by the tongue and the upper palate on the divine plane, and the right and left nostrils on the spiritual plane. Therefore, when we chant, we unite the masculine and feminine principles, which are contained in the mouth.

Although we all eat, drink, speak and sing, few people have ever really understood the importance of the mouth. Like God, the activity of the mouth never ceases—from the first cry of life to our last breath. In actuality, prayer and chanting are very divine ways to use the mouth. Through chanting, we cause the energy to move up the larynx, and as the larynx expresses itself through the mouth, which combines the two principles, then once again, we regain our power through our wholeness. In other words, mantra allows us to channel our energies upward to animate the larynx and take care of the divine centers, referred to as the pituitary and pineal glands. After practice, our speech becomes one with the Logos—the creative word—and then we become all-powerful.

What is the Logos? The Logos is the 22 forces by which the world was created. They are symbolized by the 22 letters of the Hebrew alphabet. The Logos is not only the language of the heart and soul, but also it is universally understood by all creatures. The Logos is the Christic principle, and all beings of light communicate through it. For example, thought, speech and the written word are the trinity which allows us to manifest the Logos. When we use our speech to heal, uplift and strengthen other beings, the Logos starts manifesting in us, and the forces of nature start to obey us. The Logos is the sequence of which speech is the consequence. The choice of words to express a thought is called speech. It is used on the physical plane to communicate with those who speak the same language. Although the Logos can be expressed through speech, the latter has a lot of imperfections.

We talk to God through the Logos, and the Logos belongs to the world of spirit. A proper use of sound creates a merger with the Logos. Mantra is the Logos in action. To apply this action in our lives is to take the first step on the spiritual path.

I have seen thousands of people under my guidance experience the wonders of chanting in their lives. I can honestly attest to its transformational effects. I extensively use chanting in my life and work. Most people do not understand the power behind it; they actually think it is weird to chant until they have a first-hand experience. Chanting is completely different from singing. It is not only an expression of divine truth, but also it goes far beyond the literal meaning of the words. We exercise for the physical body, we breathe for the mind, and we chant for the soul.

Chanting mantras is an ideal form of union. It is the best form of tantric, because it allows one to capture the unity of the Logos. By chanting, we not only activate the divine glands, but also we harmonize the Logos with the vocal cords and the larynx, making the latter the seat of our creative powers. Chanting makes you bright and beautiful. The radiance and beauty of a person depends on the glow and clarity of their electromagnetic field, which in turn depends on the balance of energy in their masculine and feminine principle. This allows us to become a magnet to what we need. Most importantly, our speech coincides with the Logos, and as a result we develop the omnipotence of the two principles in our larynx. Then, we are able to command the forces of nature and become truly creative, in expressing our divinity.

The divine light is within, longing for you to connect. It is your decision to access this gift. It takes patience and concentration, but the rewards are immense.

Healing Sounds for Relationships and Life

THE HEALING MANTRA:
RA MA DA SA SA SAY SO HUNG

Ra Ma Da Sa Sa Say So Hung is called the *Shushmana Mantra*. It contains the eight sounds that stimulate the Kundalini to flow in the central channel of the spine and in the spiritual centers. This sound balances the five zones of the left and right hemispheres of the brain to activate the neutral mind. As this happens, the hypothalamus pulsates in rhythm with the divine gland, causing the pituitary master gland to tune the entire glandular system. Then the sympathetic, parasympathetic and autonomic nervous systems match the timing of the glandular system. As a result, the muscular system and cells in the blood work in conjunction to receive this healing vibration, and the rebuilding process of one's health is triggered.

This mantra, which is set to a healing classical tune, can purify the aura and consolidate your mental projection into a one-pointed positivity towards yourself and your health. Listening to it helps rebalance the entire auric circulation and gives you a sense of security that activates your self-healing capacities. A consistent listening or chanting practice becomes impressive enough to permeate the subconscious, which in turn automatically influences the conscious mind. Then it becomes a part of one's deep intuitional conviction.

Ra Ma Da Sa is like a rare diamond, which connects you with the pure healing energy of the universe. You can instill the health trend in your consciousness by injecting this strong healing vibration into your mind. Then your actions and whole being will obey that thought. In order to change health troubles, we must alter the process of thought that brings the crystallization of consciousness into different forms of matter and action. This recording helps you develop the pattern of health.

RA—the fire principle—symbolizes the Sun. There would be no life on earth if it were not for the Sun showering us with the pranic life-force. Working with the Sun is the highest practice of Kabbalah.

The Sun is a source of energy, life and warmth. In other words, the Sun is the heart of our universe. It purifies and energizes.

MA—the water principle—is the energy of the Moon. MA calls on the cosmos through the sound of compassion, causing the universe to become the mother and you the child, and this brings you help and healing. It is cooling and nurturing.

DA—the earth principle—provides the ground of action.

SA—the air principle—is the impersonal infinity. When sound takes place in the external plane, it becomes "A", which represents manifestation.

The first part of the mantra expands toward heaven. By repeating the sound SA as a turning point, it causes the spirit to descend from above into matter in order to animate and vitalize it with healing and life. In other words, the second part of the mantra brings the healing qualities of the superior world back down to the earth. The last stanza of the emerald tablet from the great Hermes Trismegistus, which reveals the secret of healing and order in the material plane, is followed in this mantra. It reads, "Ascend with great sagacity from earth to heaven, and then again descend to earth, and unite together the powers of things superior and inferior. Thus you will obtain the glory of the whole world and obscurity will fly away from you. The secret is adaptation, transforming one thing into another thing." *Ra Ma Da Sa Sa Say So Hung* transforms an unbalanced and unhealthy body into a harmonious, healthy one. As in the Star of David—a symbol of two interlaced triangles—this mantra interlinks spirit with matter.

After SA comes SAY, which is the totality of experience. SO is the personal sense of identity. HUNG is the infinite, vibrating and real. HUNG suggests *Hu*, which is the life of God in every thing and every being. The *ng* causes the sound in HUNG to stimulate the divine glands. The sound of the breath is SO HUNG. The inhale is SO and the exhale is HUNG. The two qualities of SO HUNG together mean "I am Thou." As you chant this mantra, you expand toward the infinite and merge back with the finite. Most people have forgotten that their essence is with the infinite, unlimited creative power of the cosmos. When a person goes within himself and consciously experiences his own beauty, he touches his divinity. Then he can reunite his destiny to his highest potential.

A regular listening practice is not only good for practical, pre-ventative self-healthcare, but also it will aid in the assurance of a healthier life. It can help preserve the body and pave the way toward a positive mental projection.

Chanting or listening to this mantra set to a classical tune will drive out depression and revibrate your life. It is timeless and can not be outdated. It has worked in the past, it works now, and it will work in the future. There is no time, no place, no space and no condition attached to this mantra. It burns the seed of disease. Use it everyday. Offer it to anyone. If you work with it, it will work for you. In moments of anxiety, despair, fear or worry, let it be your safeguard. It will give you a strong sense of your own centeredness.

This mantra is a pure divine thought. When you think pure thoughts and are mentally strong, you cannot suffer the painful effects of bad karma or disease. A regular practice of listening to a CD recording of *Ra Ma Da Sa*, or chanting along with it, is like pray-ing unceasingly. When you continuously pray and meditate, you enter the land of Light, where all troubles disappear.

In the words of Yogi Bhajan, master of White Tantric and Kundalini yoga, who openly taught this healing mantra in the Western world, "It has worked for three thousand, four thousand years, why should it not work now?"

A musical recording of this mantra may be obtained through Rootlight, Inc. Please see the back of the book for details.

Position:
Sit in easy pose with your spine straight. Place your palms facing each other at the level of the navel about 6 inches apart. Concentrate on the space between the hands. Your eyes should be closed and focused at the third eye, the point between the eyebrows.

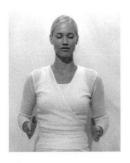

Mantra:
Inhale as deeply as possible with as much prana as you can, so that the sound may be supercharged with the subtle breath energy. On the exhale chant either up the major scale (as in *Do Re Mi Fa So La Ti Do*) or in the simple tune below either acapella or with the Rootlight recording.

To chant this mantra properly, you must remember to move the mouth fully with each sound in order to feel the vibration in the mouth and particularly the sinus areas. Feel the sound throughout the whole body. Let your mind tune into the qualities expressed by each of the eight healing sounds.

RA MA DA SA SA SAY SO HUNG

Time:
Chant aloud for 11 minutes, working up to 31. To end, take a minute or more of absolute silence and stillness to savor the experience and consolidate your energy.

OVERCOMING CHALLENGES IN RELATIONSHIPS: TRIPLE MANTRA

This is a world of duality and a place of uncertainty. We came here as spirits to have a human experience. During our stay on earth, our thoughts, feelings and actions bring into play the reaction of the laws of nature upon us and everyone in our surroundings. Negative mental attitudes and irresponsible behavior can lead to unnecessary struggles and for example, problems in relationships. Thus the deeds of the past are the karma of the present, the same way the present will become the cause of a future effect.

Everything happens according to time and space. You cannot stop time, but you can gain or lose space. The magnitude of the magnetic frequency of the earth must be neutral at a certain longitude and latitude to terminate the life of a human and dispense the five elements—earth, air, water, fire and ether. The process is similar for adversity and calamity. By vibrating *Triple Mantra*, the time may be the same, but you will not be in the space of the calamity or death. So if some earthly disturbance were to happen in a particular space, it would happen before you get there or after you are away. Adversity is the result of karma.

The truth is, the human spirit is above karma. *Triple Mantra* liberates you from the grip of karma and allows you to minimize the debt that you have incurred in the past when you were not so aware. It shifts time and space and takes you to the summit of your being, allowing you to turn unpleasant situations around. We all have debts to pay, but we must not let that be an obstacle. In the midst of challenges, keep playing or chanting *Triple Mantra* until you have reached stable ground.

This sound vibration clears all types of psychic and physical obstacles in one's daily life. It is a sure protection against car, plane or other accidents. It will strengthen your magnetic field and keep negativity out of your relationship. This mantra cuts through all opposing vibrations, thoughts, words and actions. Chanting the first part of this mantra gives you space, which means that your aura protects you by 9 feet. If you are early or late by 9 feet, you may not be entangled with that moment in time of a particular event. The second part of the mantra, starting with *ad such*, will remove obstacles from your spiritual path. The third part will remove all types of obstacles from your daily life.

Triple Mantra prevents the creation of an environment favorable to the fruition of karma that may challenge your relationship. It expands your mind, so that you may rise beyond the limitation of time and space. It renders the mind like steel and helps you develop such mental power that you start to stand unshaken no matter what comes, bravely facing anything in life.

TRIPLE MANTRA:	MEANING:
Ad Guray Nameh	*Hail to the Primal Light*
Jugad Guray Nameh	*Hail to the Light throughout the ages*
Sat Guray Nameh	*Hail to the True Light*
Siri Guru Devay Nameh	*Hail to the Transparent Light*
Ad Such	*It was true in the beginning*
Jugad Such	*True through the ages*
Hehbee Such	*And true even now*
Nanaka O-See Bee Such	*Nanak shall ever be true*

Ad Such
Jugad Such
Hehbeh Such
Nanaka O-See Beh Such

Position:
Sit in easy pose with your spine straight. Press your hands together, palm to palm in prayer pose, thumbs touching the sternum. Your eyes should be closed and focused at the third eye.

Time: Chant aloud for 11 minutes, working up to 31. To end, take a minute or more of absolute silence and stillness to consolidate your energy.

A recording of this mantra may be obtained through Rootlight, Inc. Please see the back of the book for details.

OPENING THE HEART: LUMEN DE LUMINE

Lumen de Lumine (pronounced lu-men day lu-meh-nay) symbolizes the ineffable presence of the supreme principle. Chanting or listening to *Lumen de Lumine* will create a communion between you and the beneficent and benevolent hosts of the superior astral world. It will connect you to the most powerful and protective egregore of the Kabbalists of Light. This mantra will provide physical protection against the ill will of other people. It is a prayer of the strongest potency, which will keep misfortune away and bring peace, love and mercy into the lives of those who chant or listen to it.

Lumen de Lumine is the only part recovered from the original Nicea Creed; the complete and original creed has been lost. The Nicene are the people who lived in the town of Nicaea near Constantinople, now known as Istanbul. Extensive use over the past 600 years by the Kabbalists of Light has empowered it on the collective psyche. As a result, it surrounds those who chant or listen to it with a blanket of light, and eats darkness from their lives. It opens the heart and brings serenity. It purifies and strengthens the aura. It will clear the energy in a room in a short time. Time has proven that holy blessings come to those who are in its company.

Lumen de Lumine	*Light from Light*
Deum de Deo	*God from God*
Lumen de Lumine	*Light from Light*
Deum Verum de Deo Vero	*True God from True God,*
	OR God by the Way of Light
Lumen de Lumine	*Light from Light*

Position:
Sit in easy pose with your spine straight. Place your right hand on your heart and your left hand on top. Your eyes should be closed and focused at the third eye point between the brows.

Time:
Chant aloud for 11 minutes, working up to 31.

The CDs *Lumen de Lumine* and *Mystic Light* with this mantra may be obtained through Rootlight, Inc. Please see the back of the book for details.

CHAPTER NINE

The Lower and Higher World

The human body has seven nerve centers called chakras, which are the reflection of the seven great positive centers of consciousness. These seven chakras work through the center of the spine as the seven archangels work through the planetary bodies. The physical location of these seven psychic centers, in ascending order, are: 1) root chakra—the rectum, 2) sex chakra—reproductive organs, 3) navel, 4) heart center, 5) throat chakra, 6) third eye—pituitary gland, and 7) crown chakra—pineal gland.

After Man's fall from the first estate, he was mixed with the corruptible matter that imprisoned his immortal spirit. Human disease, prejudice, error and vice are the consequences of the restriction of the immortal spirit. They derive from our material, animal nature. In other words, the primary origin of human corruption is the corruptible material from which we are made. Animal nature imposes its will on the transcendental, spiritual principle, causing a blind lack of understanding and errors of the heart. This condition is passed from man to man, and can therefore be aptly called hereditary corruption. Make no mistake; the corruption of which I speak is inherent. It can be found, to varying degrees, everywhere in the material world. Our animalistic nature is symbolized by the first three chakras. The upper three represent our divine or angelic side. The heart center is the balance point. In the Kabbalistic Tree of Life, the heart center is represented by Tiphareth, or the Sun, and is located at the midpoint on the central pillar.

Forty percent of humankind is stuck in the lowest chakra, known as the rectum or root chakra. It is here at this level that you will find those who are clouded with fear, insecurity and doubt. Another 30 percent are stuck at the sex chakra. Sex is the only way these people relate to others. Sometimes they do not even understand this. These people can be sexually addictive. Then, twenty percent of the population will be found at the level of the navel chakra. All they know is money, power and control. With regards to the heart chakra, you will find only five percent of the people at this level. Those people who are at the heart center love to serve, heal and uplift others. Most of the diseases, wars and natural disasters come from those who are stuck in the lower three chakras. Through gratification of their vices, some people create suffering or death for other innocent people. The feelings or thoughts of those people always disturb the spirit of the earth, water, fire and air elements. As a result, this disturbance generates changes in the atmosphere. This, in turn, creates natural catastrophes, such as scourge, incurable diseases, etc., which directly or indirectly affect all of us.

There are various mystical organizations and spiritual teachers committed to bringing those who are bound in the lower three chakras up to the heart center. The practice of service allows them to live consciously and experience kindness, compassion, charity, humanness, forgiveness, benevolence and understanding.

Automatic and unconscious living is the main source of pain and unhappiness. It is not enough to live under the umbrella of spirituality. Until you live consciously, you are not truly spiritual. By practicing awareness, you will benefit far more than one who just reads books and claims to be spiritual. Quicken your awareness by learning the laws of nature and apply them in every act, for awareness is the true art of self-healing.

Regarding Love Relationships

When you engage in a love union with someone who is stuck in the root chakra, you open yourself to their fears, doubts and insecurities. If you happen to have a weak aura and limited perception, their energy will often overpower you. As a result, you will start to see life through their eyes. Since fear and doubt weaken the aura, you open yourself to all kinds of adversity. However, if you are at the heart center and your aura is strong, it is possible to pull this partner up. *Remember, your own cup must be full before you can help someone else; otherwise you will drain each other.*

A love relationship with someone who is stuck at the sexual chakra is like descending to the level of a rabbit. All this particular partner relates to is sex. He or she often does not know that there is more to life than sex. This person is a gate to trouble. They want to have sex with most people of the opposite sex. Their illusionary happiness comes from any additional person they can add to the pile of broken hearts they collect. They irresponsibly hunt to find one more naive heart to tear. It is at the sex chakra that you will literally destroy your immune system permanently. Many incurable illnesses come through this door. At this level, your life is held by a very thin rope which can break at any time. If you are conscious enough, you can avoid this person. Otherwise you are open to more trouble than you can imagine.

If your mate is stuck at the navel chakra, you will be faced with control issues. This person can abuse you financially, physically, emotionally, and mentally. Money and power are primary to them; you are just secondary. For them, you are just an object that money can buy. The only time they come to you is when they need a break from their money-hunting. When you deal with them, it does not matter how mad they are with you. Tell them about how to save or make more money and you will be their friend.

The following meditation will help you heal self-destructive patterns.

MEDITATION: RELEASE NEGATIVE PATTERNS

TREE OF LIFE HAND SYMBOL

There is a symbol which is referred to as the Tree of Life Hand Symbol. Actually, I believe it is the most powerful Kabbalah symbol one can find. This symbol has already been empowered in the collective psyche. It is a particular formula which helps resolve one's problems in life. This symbol brings your consciousness into the moment. It changes your attitude by moving you outside of the duality of this planet into a state of oneness. It is the highest level of facing any moment. It will completely revibrate your life. We are not time and space; we flow through time and space. This flow is called the life-flow. Any mental, emotional and physical blocks in this life-flow manifest as disturbances, and if not attended to, eventually disease. Disturbance, or disharmony, is only possible when the masculine and feminine principles are out of balance.

The Tree of Life Hand Symbol corrects the flow of energy and dissolves any blocks. It will bring balance to all areas of your life. It can be used whenever you have a question or problem that needs resolution. The answer will soon come to you. It is also an effective tool to use in combination with visualization.

In this position, you are creating the three pillars of the Tree of Life. Your right hand is the Pillar of Mercy, the masculine principle; your left hand is the Pillar of Severity, the feminine principle; and you are in the middle, the Pillar of Equilibrium. This posture will take you beyond time and space into a healing space. It will connect you to the Fountain of Light, the source of all.

Position:

- Sit down in a meditative position, spine straight.

- Bring both hands to the level of your diaphragm, palms facing each other about 6 inches apart, elbows bent and relaxed.

- Meditate in this position for as long as possible. This mudra can be used to work on oneself and others. You may either put your name or someone else's name within the space between your hands, or place a mental image of yourself or another in the space for healing.

Mantra:

From personal experience, I have found that chanting a mantra in this posture is very effective. I recommend that you chant the following healing mantra:

RA MA DA SA SA SAY SO HUNG

These eight healing vibrations cut through time and space and heal the mind, body and spirit. It maintains, strengthens and improves your health. Inhale deeply and chant up the major scale on the exhale. You may also chant along with a CD recording of this mantra. *See page 66 for a complete description.*

Ra	*Sun*
Ma	*Moon*
Da	*Earth*
Sa	*Infinity*
Sa	*Infinity*
Say So Hung	*I am thou*

Time:
Continue for 5–11 minutes.

Wisdom is born of truth,
and truth exists all around us, waiting
to be incorporated into our lives.
It is in the heart alone that we can
easily find this truth and are
able to decipher all mysteries.

CHAPTER TEN

The Heart Center
and Relationships

It is easier for God to work through an open heart than one that is closed. One can create a platform for a healing and joyful relationship by staying centered in the heart. When the heart is closed, things can be quite difficult in a love relationship. The difference between spiritual-man and animal-man lies with the heart and the head. Those who operate from the heart, operate from a place of spiritual clarity. Those who operate from the head, however, operate from a place of intellectual confusion. They have lost their most powerful form of protection, and the wheels of life grind them to powder. This is evidenced by the fact that the intellectual, scientific and cultural achievements of man have not furthered our heart's evolution. They have merely covered the fundamental animal instinct of mankind with a fine coating of sophistication and civilization. The heart is our bridge to the Divine, as it is connected to grace, healing, intuition, wisdom and truth. Wisdom is born of truth, and truth exists all around us, waiting to be incorporated into our lives. It is in the heart alone that we can easily find this truth and are able to decipher all mysteries.

In order to rise above your animal nature and stop the cycle of endless modification of animal instincts, you need to open your heart. As long as Man lives from the corruptible, material essence expressed through the three lower chakras, there can be no hope for higher happiness and peace. The heart must be your one and only guide. When you open your heart, you change the mortal to immortal, the corruptible to incorruptible. You subjugate your animal nature so that all thoughts, words and deeds are initiated from a place of love, light and truth. Just as each ray of the sun is a source of energy, each thought, word or deed that comes from the heart positively contributes to those around us, including our love partner. Life is sustained and nourished.

The heart is the innermost sanctuary and the holiest of temples. Its fire is the heavenly light that will warm up your love relationship. It is the only vehicle for reuniting with God. As you discover the light of your heart, you will experience profound changes in your love relationship, career and life. For those who have awakened the heart's holy flame are content and free, even in restricting conditions. These individuals see straight through to the core of all matters. The foundation and inevitability of human corruption becomes apparent. However, in spite of the corruption that is discovered, these individuals strive to aid the fallen and assist those who have gone astray. They do not succumb to hopelessness, but rather seek to better that which they can.

The heart center is the home of the conscious principle and the seat of prana. Prana is life. The heart is the source of manifestation, the seat of life and the medium between man and God. It maintains the existence of the physical body. Prana resides in the area from the nostrils to the lungs. Situated in the cavity of the mouth, prana allows food to pass through to the stomach, and its location near the heart preserves life from destruction. Prana further acts to regulate the other elements of the body, effectively keeping them in balance. With the help of prana, we are able to move, see, think and hear.

The heart center is governed by the element of air, known as *vayu*. The element air is tactile. Air is the protective element in the body. It is the vital force that keeps the organs healthy and the blood circulating. The heart or fourth chakra rules the chest region, known as vayu-granthi, including: the lungs, heart, thymus, cell producers and all their subsidiaries. When you are in possession of strong vayu-granthi, self-control, balanced temperament, purity of thought and unselfishness are yours.

The heart center is the most important of your spiritual centers. It is one of the two centers which are in direct contact with the higher self and through which soul energy and the other higher energies enter our being. The second entrance is the head center whose location is in almost the exact center of the head in the vicinity of the pineal gland.

As previously discussed, Ojas, which is the essential energy of the body, exists on a subtle level in the heart chakra from where it pervades the entire body, giving stability and support. Ojas is the ultimate essence of the reproductive system and all vital secretions, and the heat of the tissues. Ojas is not a physical substance; it is the sap of our life energy and the essential energy of the immune system. When Ojas is sufficient there is health; when it is deficient there is disease. Health problems will come to us in the parts of the body where the Ojas is low. When it is destroyed, one dies, and when it is sustained, one lives.

From a Chinese medical point of view, the heart is affected by anxiety and excess joy and passion. When these intense emotions are not rooted in pure balance, they are detrimental to the Ojas, as they burn yin. Yin is the water-like substance that composes our flesh. Any intense emotion, such as anger, stress, excessive sexual indulgence, greed and any drive that causes us to make poor decisions and lifestyle choices, will cause premature depletion of the precious yin. When the yin becomes deficient, symptoms such as hormone deficiency, reproductive problems, fatigue, dry skin, thin bones and immune weakness arise. According to Chinese thought, the yin cannot be replaced through food or medication. The only source of yin replenishment lies in the Universal Energy itself and is built within the body through meditation.

Ojas is decreased by factors such as anger, hunger, worry, sorrow, and overwork. A lack of Ojas results in fear, constant worry or a lack of strength, which disturbs the senses. There is a general lack of color to the skin tone, the mind becomes weakened, and there is a physical wasting. Qualities such as patience and faith disappear.

On the physical level, the heart center is associated with the heart, lungs, circulatory and respiratory systems. When the heart center does not work properly, one can get heart and lung diseases, such as childhood asthma, which reflect deep-seated issues concerning identity, self-consciousness and emotion. Heart diseases include heart attacks, stroke, angina, arteriosclerosis and hypertension. Heart diseases are the main cause of heart attacks and are often preceded by palpitations, insomnia, numbness or severe pain in the chest or middle back that radiates down the arms. Causes of heart diseases include inappropriate diet, physical or emotional trauma, congenital or hereditary factors, suppressed emotions or excess strain or anxiety.

The first thing to do in order to heal the heart involves an extended period of rest or reduced activity, both physical and mental. Strain and worry must be set aside. Heavy exercise and travel should be avoided. Sufferers of diseases such as anemia, hypertension, palpitations, tuberculosis, asthma and bronchitis may concentrate on their heart center while performing asanas and other yogic techniques.

Most people die of broken hearts or spiritual starvation. People suffering from heart diseases need to make it a top priority to get in touch with their true hearts and what they really want to do in life.

The heart chakra acts as the balancing point between the three lower chakras and the three higher chakras. From the fourth chakra, energy flows both downward and upward. Female and male energies merge. The desires of the lower triangle are calmed. One turns his attention toward the pursuit of higher aims. The emotional self evolves and the cosmic mind is accessed.

People who vibrate at the fourth chakra operate with a heightened level of compassion. They communicate with words that are honest and kind, and speak only to please the soul and consciousness of others. Indeed, they speak from the heart. The drawback of the fourth chakra is the tendency to focus too much time and energy on rectifying what was. One must show compassion to oneself, as well as others. A closed fourth chakra signifies a general lack of compassion.

The heart brings you grace and grace takes away temptation, anger, lust, greed, unvirtuous and unrighteous living. By living through the heart, you relate to your spirit and flow of the soul and you feel the total divinity within. It is a manifestation of divinity. It is through the fourth chakra that a person becomes aware of the seven negative karmic influences, the behavioral patterns of his life.

The heart, or fourth chakra, is the central chakra and is influenced by the higher and lower forces simultaneously. Therefore, one must be very careful to balance the energies of the heart. Be aware that passion is truly an enemy of the heart, inciting pain, betrayal, deceit and lies. A heart consumed by passion is ruled by anger, jealousy and negativity. There are two doors in the heart of man: through the lower door, human beings can give passion access to the heart's elementary light, which can only be attained through this route. Passion creates a hell within the human heart that is so removed from heaven, that it becomes very difficult to remember one's connection with God. One of the main things people suffer from is anger, and it is through this lower door that you find this destructive fire. A heart enslaved by passion is so consumed by ego that it cannot recognize the words of the soul, and thus cannot ask God to preside within its depths.

Through the higher door human beings may give the spirit access to divine light, which can only be communicated here on Earth through this channel. Here one receives divine grace through the understanding, knowledge and application of cosmic principles. When the heart is pure in spirit, the individual feels at one with the presence of divinity, and is able to perceive divine grace in all things. This connection to the divine surpasses mere intellectual understanding and infuses the individual with the oneness of life through the heart.

When one vibrates exclusively in the three lower chakras, it is very difficult to develop a positive attitude. However, vibrating from the heart center causes a person to develop good habits, by attuning his own vibratory rate with that of the universe. Working with the heart and breath allows one simultaneous control over the breath patterns and the heart, creating positive vibratory frequencies. A good attitude in turn helps develop the heart center; each wrong breath is an injury to the organism. Furthermore, we increase our positive attitudes by working closely with the seven creative planets and the laws of the universe as revealed in the book *Lifting the Veil*. One can dramatically improve one's life by rising before dawn to pray, chant or meditate.

Pure habits and truly nourishing food cause the mind and body to become pure and clear. The practice of good habits helps a person stabilize his existence, so that his energy flows rhythmically in a positive direction away from the life-depleting distractions of the lower chakras.

In truth, one can open the heart by working with the divine spiritual wisdom herein revealed, as well as in the following books: *The Divine Doctor, Lifting the Veil,* and *The Healing Fire of Heaven.* For the heart is a temple of spiritual wisdom and truth, an inner sanctuary that arose after the fall of man. God, through this temple, reveals how man can, once again, regain his former dignity and release himself from misery. Sacred wisdom is the vehicle whereby divine power is imparted. **The heart's wisdom is a depository of knowledge, both knowledge of mankind and the ancient mysteries. Therefore, the heart is the true center of light, and it is in this light that we find the key to our wisdom.** By mastering the heart chakra, the voice becomes softer and gentler as one starts to speak from the heart. One's voice penetrates the heart of others, and thus without any exertion of power, the opened-hearted person attracts to himself/herself a group of admirers striving to reach the same vibrational patterns. One becomes like Jupiter—the Lord of material and spiritual wellness, including speech. The senses are completely under control. They are dearer than the dearest to most people. Life is inspired, and poetry flows through their speech like a stream of clear water uninterrupted. Their writings are soothing and healing to the human soul. When the true yogi or Kabbalist succeeds in opening their heart center, they gain the power to become invisible and can project voluntarily anywhere they wish. Their enemies recede. The visible and invisible worlds are opened to and they become filled with the devotional spirit, referred to as *bhakti.* One begins to identify oneself with the rest of creation, bringing on a sense of cosmic unity.

By working with the heart, we are able to attune ourselves with the rhythms of the universe, and then perfect knowledge of God, Nature and Man is granted. Our heart is the reflection of the Sun in us. It is the custodian of the power of the Sun's rays, which carry illumination, light, energy and strength. The light of the heart banishes all darkness. Whosoever opens and follows the heart obtains the grace of heaven, and is delivered from sin and enjoys immunity from disease. Again, it is in the heart that you will find the light of nature, the light of reason, and the light of revelation.

The fourth chakra is the point of higher consciousness where the lower and higher selves meet. It is the storehouse of many lifetimes of experiences. Tiphareth on the Tree of Life represents the Sun in us and the heart center. It does not take much to know that the Sun is a fountain of light and energy. The attributes of light are joy, peace, love, knowledge, etc. If you apply the attributes of the Sun to your behavior with your partner, you will elevate the consciousness of the relationship. Kindness, humanness, compassion, forgiveness and service are some of the qualities associated with the heart center. When each partner invests in those qualities, the relationship blossoms.

As an individual, you vibrate at one frequency and your partner vibrates at another. When you are together, you make a frequency created by the two of you. Your goal should be to raise the frequency of the relationship; otherwise it will sink into the lower world. Once this happens, it becomes difficult for the couple to stay together. This is mainly due to the storm of fear, doubt, insecurities, etc., which weakens the electromagnetic field of the love relationship. All you will find in the lower world is bad weather.

As mentioned before, the heart center is the bridge between the lower and higher selves. It is the reflection of the Sun in us. Therefore, the weather is very sunny, pleasant and beautiful at that level. When both partners come from the heart, the relationship becomes centered and stable. It rises above the stormy weather experienced in the lower three chakras.

As an example: I met this nice old man at an engineering seminar. From our conversation I learned that he had been married for 37 years. Since curiosity well-directed is the law of evolution, I asked him what his secret was. This was his answer:

"My wife and I decided early in our relationship to play one game. The game is who will make the other more happy. We have been competing for many years. We are still competing. This simple game brought lots of joy and happiness to our marriage."

When each partner serves and uplifts the other, as the Sun does to all of us, the relationship moves from the storm and confusion of duality to the peace and harmony of Divinity. By serving your partner, you not only develop the ability to uplift the relationship, but also radiate more than enough magnetism to keep the union healthy. When both partners start serving each other, they automatically attract the grace of God in their lives, for God serves those who serve others. Therefore, when the couple applies the principle of service, they have the support of God. Through service, not only does the couple live like the Sun, they also generate a high vibration of love in the relationship, thereby creating powerful and positive changes on the mental, spiritual and physical levels.

All great souls that humankind has ever known have used the tool of service. If you want a happy and successful relationship, serve your partner with kindness, compassion, attention and love. By doing so, you save yourself from self-centeredness, control, greed, contempt and resentment. Refusal to serve weakens the couple's electromagnetic field and creates room for unhappiness and pain. The practice of the Divine spiritual wisdom that I share through my books, causes the heart to open and spiritual power to be granted. Harmony, known as happiness, comfort, profit and gain, is yours. Those who have opened their hearts possess a light which anoints them and by which they gain understanding of the secret aspects of nature. They are blessed and speak words of truth. They possess a fire whose flame nourishes. They are bearers of knowledge that can bind us to higher worlds, and render perceptible the sights and sounds of these higher worlds. Through perfect union with the light of the heart, the new man in us is gradually born. Divine wisdom and love unite to form a new spiritual man whose heart belief changes to reality.

Open yourself to your heart's wisdom and guidance, and it will start working for the regeneration and resurrection that loosens the bonds of impure and corruptible matter, and releases you from a life of repression and powerlessness. Christ spoke of the mysteries of regeneration. Indeed, God reaches his most beloved through the heart, and dispatches them to help establish the order that seeks to aid in the evolution of human nature so that misery is healed. Walk the heart's path toward happiness, redemption, faith and blessings. This is the path of the mystic.

MEDITATION TO OPEN AND HEAL THE HEART

I Am, also known as *I Am That I Am*, is a powerful spiritual formula that establishes a connection between the chanter and God—Holy Father, Almighty and Merciful One, Who has created all things, Who knows all things and can do all things, from Whom nothing is hidden, to Whom nothing is impossible. It is the One who allows you to penetrate the knowledge of hidden things and understand their secret nature. Through *I Am*, we receive aid from the Most Holy ADONAI, whose Kingdom and Power shall have no end unto the Ages of the Ages.

I Am is the revelation that Moses had in the burning bush. In the desert at the burning bush "the angel of the LORD appeared to Moses in a blazing fire from the midst of the bush, and identified Himself clearly." Moses said to God, "Suppose I go to the Israelites and say to them, 'The God of your fathers has sent me to you,' and they ask me, 'What is His Name?' Then what shall I tell them?" God said to Moses, "I Am That I Am."

"I Am That I Am" is also what Jesus meant when he said, my Father and I are One. It is the Holy Name of God, EHEIEH. This name is the root, source, and origin of all the other Divine Names, from whence they draw their life and virtue. It is the name Adam invoked in order to acquire knowledge of all created things. It contains the power, wisdom, and virtue of the Spirit of God. The vast mercy and strength of God manifests in the life of those who work with it.

While *I Am* looks very simple, it conceals a mighty force that takes effect when awakened in the soul. It connects you with your own spiritual force. This connection creates internal harmony and protection that extends to every aspect of your life. In order to work effectively with the mantra *I Am*, you must fill your entire inner being with its words by inhabiting their meaning with the full strength of your soul. Know that as you meditate on *I Am*, you become existence itself, without form, quality, past, present or future. In other words, this mantra relates the finite identity of the first I am with the infinite identity of the second I am. The first I am, then, is the personal reference. The second I am relates the I of self-identity to the Am of the existence of being.

A consistent, daily practice of chanting *I Am* will connect you to the higher world. You must display patience to practice this meditation day by day, over and over again, for a long time. If you have this patience, then, after some time, you will notice a thought arising within you—no longer a mere concept but a thought thriving with life and force. Soon, this thought will reveal itself to you as if it were radiating light. Within this inner radiation of light, you will feel bountiful, blissful, happy and full of the joy of existence. A feeling will then permeate you. This feeling can only be described as joyful love in creative existence. A force imparts itself to the will as if the thought was radiating warmth through the will, energizing it. You can garner all of this by merging with the *I Am*. You will gradually realize that, by sinking into the *I Am*, the highest intellectual, psychic, and moral powers are birthed in you.

I Am is a powerful way to reconnect with your true center, so that you may experience love, peace, and true joy in your life. Meditating on *I Am* with dedication, while chanting along with the Rootlight *Sounds of the Ether* CD* will initiate an integration of your mind, body, and spirit that enables you to unravel the mystery of your own being. In turn, you will come to unravel the understanding and nature of God. Indeed, as this mantra becomes firmly fixed in the mind, all restrictive bonds and limitations are removed. Your sense of personal relatedness to the cosmic will be heightened, as you are connected with the healing energy of the universe and showered with angelic gifts and blessings. This mantra is the essence of truth and the nature of reality. Chanting and/or listening to it will connect you with the higher world and surround you with the beneficial light of heaven. Use it to feel the heavenly connection through the God of your heart.

---

*A CD recording of I AM That I AM can be found on *Sounds of the Ether,* available through Rootlight, Inc. For order information, please see the back of the book.

- Start by placing your palms on your chest, feeling their warmth over your heart.
- Take a few slow, deep breaths, releasing mental and physical tension with each exhale and directing your consciousness into your heart center.
- Chant "*I AM That I AM*" for 11 to 31 minutes.

PRAYER FOR A LOVE MATE

There is nothing more healing than praying for your love mate. Prayer is a gift from heaven, and a grace which is given to us by the most high. It is the great mystery, and to those who understand the use of the heart center, prayer can enable them to receive the highest influences in action on the divine level. As one mystic says, prayer is an ineffable act, because it does not claim to be anything, yet it can do everything. Prayer transforms all misfortunes into delights, because it is the daughter of love. A prayer of love is the most potent of all prayers. Love is the highest vibration. It is very pure; it is God. Where there is love, there is no fear or doubt. Where there is fear and doubt, there is no God. Love penetrates and transforms everything in the material and spiritual matrix. Those who dwell in love dwell in God.

Prayer is a matter of the heart, not the head. By praying for your love mate, you are praying for yourself as well. The Godly energy expresses itself through colors as well. Light pink is the color of love. That pink looks like the beautiful pink glow of sunset.

- Sit in a meditative position, spine straight, head erect, hands resting on your lap. Take a few moments to quiet the mind and slow the breath.
- Visualize a beautiful light-pink flame in the center of your being or at your heart. With every breath, see it progressively expand and surround you with this beautiful sphere of light-pink energy.

◆ Feel love, warmth and kindness radiating from that pink flame in your heart center, permeating every cell and spreading into your sphere of energy.

◆ Now, in your mind's eye, imagine your love mate at his or her best and smiling.

◆ Inhale some of that pink light. As you exhale, send it to him or her. See this cloud of beautiful protective light completely envelop your mate.

◆ Take a deep breath, hold, then exhale as you whisper *"It is done."*

◆ Now quickly dismiss all thoughts about it. If you still hold to the thought, it is like writing a letter that you do not want to mail. You cannot receive an answer if you don't send it. It is only after you mail that letter and dismiss the thought of the answer or result of the letter, that it will come to you. This is true for all visualization.

Comments:

This prayer will bring you spiritual strength and elevate your consciousness. You will be more in tune with yourself and your surroundings, and communication between the two of you will improve. Prayer is the essence. It is the projection that turns fate into destiny. All power comes from prayers.

CHAPTER ELEVEN

Communication and Love Relationships

Communication is critical to the success, growth and enhance-ment of a love relationship. All it takes is one wrong word to inflict a wound that will destroy a promising love relationship. In the same way the right word, said at the right time, with the right tone can heal, uplift and strengthen a love relationship.

Our consideration for others is what distinguishes human beings from other animals. We express this consideration, or lack thereof, in the manner in which we use our words. Indeed, words are the most common and effective tool of human interaction. Your words are living things, sparked into creation by the energy of the heart, mind and spirit. They carry the energy of your thoughts directly into the physical or material realm. Words, then, are manifested thoughts whose energy vibrates more in line with this reality. Words create a ripple effect whose reach is vast. They vibrate through the air and can be heard and felt. They are capable of initiating healing or inflicting wounds. This is especially true when we are dealing with our love partners, as they are the most sensitive and susceptible and the most open to the power of our words.

The Divine God itself created all that we know of as reality with a thought. As sparks of the Divine, we carry a similar creative poten-tial and power. It is important to let the infinite power of spirit flow through your words. The secret of tapping into this power lies in staying in close contact with the eternal source. Always speak with a heart full of gratitude. Remember that a grateful heart is an open heart, and it is much easier for Light to work through an open heart than one that is closed. Continually give thanks for everything that you are and everything that you have. In this way, God will work in and through you to bring about the wonders and glory of heaven.

Words hold tremendous transformative power. There are words for healing and comfort, words that uplift, words that empower, and words that attract blessings. Conversely, there are words that destroy. Words can then, be used to either enhance or destroy a love relationship. Communication is much more than idle, non-reflective, unconscious chatter. It is the art of using one's voice. When we choose to use our voice and words in a constructive, positive manner, we are engaged in the art of communication rather than the mere act of speaking. When communication is perfected, it becomes harmonious. When using harmonious communication one is aware of its impact on both the giver and receiver. When love partners engage in harmonious communication, they merge the spheres of intelligence, consciousness and heart, thereby creating the atmosphere for success; an atmosphere in which healthy compromises are made, disagreements are resolved, and both partners are supported. A beautiful symphony of words removes the seeds of disharmony and bad luck, and rewrites the couple's destiny.

To be sure, harmonious communication has nothing to do with what you want, feel or know. Compassion, honesty and kindness are the keys to harmonious communication. In order to transform the mere act of speaking into an act of harmonious communication that heals the soul and consciousness of your partner, you must learn how to think and feel for him/her in order to be able to relate to them effectively. In other words, you must learn how to walk a mile in your partner's shoes in order to reach your partner in a very healthy way. When communicating harmoniously, you are relating to both the knowledge you have of your partner, as well as the knowledge you wish to convey. This is done in the most healing and loving of ways, with all offensiveness, criticism, judgment and condemnation banished from your repertoire of speech. You let love and

understanding pour from you, and expect the best from your partner. Remember, love transforms all bitterness and hatred.
Understanding can open even the most closed, cold and unrespon-
sive of hearts. When you are able to empathize with your partner,
you are able to communicate in a manner that serves to strengthen
the union. Harmonious communication that positively influences
your love relationship is dependent upon an open throat center. Both
you and your partner can open this center by chanting along with
the mantras offered on our sacred music CD series.

The throat center, known as the fifth chakra, is located in the
throat area at the junction of the medulla oblongata. Comprised of
the space between the collarbone and the nape of the neck, the fifth
chakra is known as the *vyana-granthi* region. Its color is smoky purple,
and it is governed by ether. The throat center, or fifth chakra, is the
center of creative expression, and relates to the ability to communicate directly. This is the arena of knowledge that lies beyond the
senses. Here, negative, positive and neutral life breathes, apana, prana
and vyana coexist. It is also the domain of the thyroid, parathyroid,
salivary glands and tonsils. The secretions produced by these glands
help to mold and nourish our minds. A person with a predominance
of vyana-granthi possesses a mind that is in tune with supreme consciousness. With an intellect free from the impurity of worldly
pursuits, he/she is able to see the past, present and future within.
He/she has knowledge of the world beyond the senses. Gentleness,
steadiness, modesty, mercy and courage—the calling cards of harmonious communication—are also his/her calling cards. There is
freedom from expectation, both positive and negative. Compassion
is the hallmark. Ultimately, he/she strives to share with others how
they have confronted and conquered their karma. This is not done
in an authoritarian manner, rather, the qualities of harmonious communication described here are employed.

When your throat center works properly, you utter the words
that live in the heart and mind for generations to come. When this
center does not work for you, however, you cannot create a positive
utterance, no matter what your intention is. You wish to speak but
cannot. Again, if the partners in a love relationship cannot speak to one

another, sharing both their joys and concerns in a constructive manner, their relationship will be beset with difficulties. It cannot be stressed enough that communication is the most powerful ingredient in life and love. A low level of consciousness is revealed in the partner who is unable to maintain harmonious speech and the patience required for effective delivery. Again, the majority of the problems we encounter in our love relationships are due to poor communication skills. Indeed, those who do not develop the art of harmonious communication are laying the foundation for a life of difficulty in love, as their deficiency renders the positive power of communication null and void.

The qualities that produce the harmony in your soul that can be projected outward to your partner, via your words, are gentleness, mildness, respect, humility, modesty, tolerance and forgiveness. Conversely, arrogance, wrath, vice, attachment, greed, and jealousy are the qualities that produce the disharmony in your soul that can be projected outward to your partner, via your words. These qualities are all tied to ego, and ego, the ultimate creator of disharmony, becomes increasingly powerful when indulged. For a time ego may be satisfied by the gratification it receives, but soon it needs more in order to garner satisfaction. A love relationship ruled by the ego quickly becomes a burden. Indeed, the destructive process of inharmonious thought and speech is responsible for all the chaos, turmoil, and loss of hope we encounter in our love relationships and life. In order to avoid this, it is imperative that those who walk the spiritual path refrain from dwelling in the negativity that can impair your union. Do not create negativity or feed any that exists. Realize that as a spiritual person, your thoughts and words are powerful because the spiritual forces that flow and work through them are heightened in their strength. Therefore, the negative thoughts or words of one on the spiritual path will speed up the creation and manifestation of negative outcomes.

When you speak, your words are remembered in the same way you remember what has been said to you. Despite the many other wonderful qualities you may possess, aggressive and/or unpleasant speech will work against you in affairs of the heart. The negative mind is the first mind that receives speech. Painful words release related memories in the subconscious. Therefore, when you speak inharmoniously to your partner, his/her mind goes on alert, ready to defend itself against attack. You have initiated a tide of negativity that you must now contend with. It is likely that you have polluted, in small or large measure, the future of the relationship, even though your partner may try his/her best to remain positive in the face of negative communication. Remember that love relationships require the healing exchange of harmonious communication as well as caring. You must be willing, via the art of communication, to create a positive atmosphere in which your love can grow.

Sometimes we behave as if our love relationship were the perfect arena for venting past and present frustrations, hurts, angers and insecurities. This could not be farther from the truth. You must honor your partner and your love relationship. When you speak in order to control your partner, introduce your particular motive or assert what you want at all costs, you are wasting your communicative energy. In affairs of the heart, your words must have a healing purpose, a theme to convey and a graceful delivery. Avoid the inappropriate words, ill-advised timing and poor manners that result from anger, hurt, insecurity and ego. These states of being have no place in harmonious communications, and therefore no place in love relationships. While you may be tempted to speak when you are feeling emotionally negative and/or ego-driven, refrain until you have had a chance to rebalance yourself. In this way, you will be communicating for the future, rather than the past or present.

Even as we consciously strive to create a harmonious love relationship via the positive power of harmonious communication, careless speech happens. Many times we reveal our limitations, narrowness, or small mindedness by speaking words that were better left unsaid. Recognize when you have spoken to your partner in a careless manner, and quickly counteract the impending damage with the light of positive truths. That is, use the words that follow inharmonious speech to responsibly and constructively transform the negativity you may have created. Again, this will help to promote peace, growth and change in your union.

The true yogi and/or Kabbalist must train both his voice and his ear to be in tune with the harmony of life. Chanting is not only the shortest path to spiritual heights, but also it will help you develop a healing voice. When you master sound through chanting, the sound of your voice becomes a living entity. Once enlivened, your voice can be used to help you produce positive outcomes.

Chanting trains your voice, so that you are able to use the tools of hearing and speech to tune into the harmony of life. It allows you to become conscious about each word spoken, and the manner in which it is spoken. In order to create a lasting love relationship via the art of harmonious communication, it is imperative that you master the various aspects and applications of words. Remember, communication is an art, much like music. For every word there is a certain note, for every speech a proper pitch. Recognize those times when you should speak softly, loudly, or not at all. Silence is, in fact, quite precious. There are times when it is just important to Be. It provides you with time to connect with your own healing space so you may recharge yourself and then you are able to share the best of yourself with your partner.

We have already discussed how choosing the correct mode of expression is crucial to a lasting love relationship. You must also, however, regulate the speed of that expression, maintain the rhythm of the conversation and consider the level of your voice. Indeed, the true yogi and/or Kabbalist avoids all actions that lack rhythm. Let patience control the rhythm of your speech. Watch for the appropriate time to shift subjects. Do not be abrupt. Be flexible in your communication with your partner. Exercise control by waiting patiently for your partner to finish his/her thoughts. When it is your turn to speak, rein in your thoughts so that they do not stumble, willy-nilly, from your mouth. Emphasize important words. By taking your time, you will keep pace with the rhythm of the given conversation and remain coherent. Remember, only the foolish person remains as an unchangeable note. The intelligent person is flexible like a pliable note. The prideful love partner will quarrel with his/her mate. The wise and intelligent love partner, on the other hand, will re-frame his/her convictions in a way that is in harmony with the given conversation/situation.

When you speak to your partner how is the level of your voice? Is it soft or loud? There will be times when the voice is naturally softer and others when the voice is naturally louder. Voice level demonstrates the natural condition of the spirit at a particular moment. Sometimes the spirit is tender. Tenderness of the spirit is accompanied by tenderness of the voice. Sometimes the spirit becomes harder. Hardness of the spirit is accompanied by hardness in the voice. For example, the voice becomes hard naturally when we are scolding someone. Similarly, you need not soften your voice in order to show sympathy, gratitude, love, devotion, or affection. Your voice will naturally soften in accordance with these feelings before you can even think about it. This is evidence that the voice is the expression of the spirit. Again, these conditions of voice occur without conscious thought. If the spirit is soft, the voice is soft. If the spirit is hard, the voice is hard. If the spirit is powerful, the voice is powerful. If, however, the spirit has lost its vigor, the voice will also lose its vigor. Inspiration is unique in this sense as it chooses its own voice. You can evaluate the condition of your spirit throughout each day by consulting your voice. Approach your partner and your love relationship with constructive vigor. As you approach your partner, keep in mind that harmonious communication is served by the soft voice of the tender spirit. By extension, then, your love relationship is also served by the soft voice of the tender spirit. As you evaluate yourself in relation to your love relationship, know that the real character of a person is to be found in their speaking voice. Indeed, the voice reveals the stage of a particular person's evolution. Take care that your voice inspires even before the words you have spoken are understood by the mind of your partner.

Above all, you must use your words and thoughts responsibly and constructively in order to promote hope, peace, growth and a positive change in your love relationship. I am not suggesting here that you ignore the reality of your love relationship. Indeed, it is important that you see it clearly so that you are able to gather your strength to neutralize any existing negativity and make it right. No love relationship is a dream world of perfection and bliss. We all bring our karmic baggage into the love relationships we engage in. Therefore, darkness exists. Do not succumb to the darkness, however. Do not allow yourself to be controlled by it. Rather, acknowledge the light of truth and decide to use your positive will in the service of hopeful and loving transformation.

Remember that in all aspects of life, including romantic love, like attracts like. Those who are negative will attract negativity and darkness. Those who speak of violence will lead violent lives. Those who speak of sadness will live in sadness. Those who talk of pain will be inflicted with it. Conversely, those who are positive will attract that which is positive and full of Light. Those who speak of joy will live in joy. Those who talk of love will be infused by it. Control your thoughts and words through the divine spiritual wisdom that we share. Master the process of your mind. Make your love relationship a platform for spiritual growth and a healthy life.

The Thyroid and Your Health

Note to the Reader: The following section on the thyroid contains an in-depth overview of the function of the thyroid and adrenal glands. It has been included for the benefit of the vast number of people affected by thyroid and adrenal imbalance. We encourage everyone to at least browse through this section and skip over the parts that are too technical to the next section entitled "Thyroid and Spirituality."

By not speaking your truth or expressing how you feel or by doing so in an unhealthy manner, you may develop thyroid abnormalities, and this may cause severe health problems. From an energetic standpoint, the thyroid and adrenal glands may have an imbalance even if the clinical lab tests show that they're functioning normally. Many doctors admit that their patients show all signs of thyroid imbalance even though the lab test results are normal. Also, those who take thyroid medication may have a reduction in the symptoms of thyroid disorder, however they will still benefit greatly from the recommendations in this book. The thyroid medications only address, to a certain degree, the physical functions of the thyroid, however the spiritual, as well as many of the physical functions are still deficient. If your thyroid is out of balance, you also need to address it nutrionally. There are many books on the market that do a good job of this. Also, because the thyroid plays a role in bone density, it is important for those with thyroid imbalance to pay extra attention to the health of the bones. (Review the bone section in *The Healing Fire of Heaven* by Joseph Micheal Levry.)

The thyroid gland is a ductless gland consisting of two lobes situated on either side of the trachea (wind-pipe), just above the collarbones. Like many glands in the human body, the thyroid is controlled by the pituitary, a pea-sized gland at the base of the brain. If we liken the body's other glands to the sections of an orchestra, the pituitary is the conductor who makes sure that the playing is smooth and harmonious. You may be well aware of the role the thyroid takes as regulator and storehouse of the body's iodine. It is the pituitary gland that produces the hormone, called Thyroid Stimulating Hormone (TSH), which stimulates the thyroid to absorb the iodine that comes into the body.

Iodine is usually introduced into the body in its salt form, iodide. Another form can be easily taken in kelp drops or by eating seaweed. The normal daily intake of iodine is 100-200 micrograms (1 million micrograms = 1 gram.) This intake is largely absorbed from the small intestine, and transported in blood plasma. (In this state, iodide is loosely attached to protein.) In addition, small amounts of iodide are secreted by the salivary glands and stomach. The kidneys excrete about two-thirds of the iodide we consume; the thyroid absorbs the remaining one-third.

It is in the thyroid gland that iodide is oxidized to an active form of iodine. The iodine then becomes attached to the amino acid called tyrosine. Iodinated tyrosine combines to form two main substances: triodothyronine and tetraiodothyronine. The latter substance is commonly referred to as thyroxin, the major hormone produced by the thyroid. Thyroxin, then, is a form of iodine in its most active, oxidized state.

An example of the wonderful and delicate balance that exists between the various organs and glands of the human body, can be observed with the hormone thyroxin. Through a process called "feedback inhibition," thyroxin regulates its own production by controlling the amount of TSH that is released by the pituitary gland. When there is a plentiful supply of thyroxin in the bloodstream, the rate of TSH production is cut back, reducing the stimulation of the thyroid gland. Conversely, when the level of thyroxin in the bloodstream falls, the TSH activity of the thyroid gland increases.

In addition to the crucial role the thyroid plays with iodine, and its cooperative function with the pituitary gland, the thyroid works closely with the adrenals as well. Working with the adrenals, the thyroid is referred to as the body's shock absorber. In this way, it helps the physical body adjust to its emotional environment.

The thyroid plays a vital role in our mental, physical and psychic well-being. A healthy thyroid indicates that a person will have a quick, delving mind. Indeed, the mind aided by normal thyroid functioning will be keen and possess the ability for rapid adjustment. While these mental qualities do not automatically connote integrity and righteousness, they do facilitate the building of strong character and morality. Conversely, a weak or malfunctioning thyroid slows mental reactions, producing dullness, a general lack of interest and an inability to deal with the problems of life. These qualities can then lead to irresponsibility and a tendency to adopt the line of least resistance.

The thyroid gland, then, greatly effects one's mental actions and reactions. In turn, the functioning of one's physical muscles and organs is also affected. Physical tiredness results from an underactive thyroid. Moreover, the thyroid gland is important psychically, as it acts as a sort of speed control for the interchange of objective and subjective impressions. It is not the place where these impressions actually change from the objective to subjective, or vice versa. Rather, it is the mechanism that controls how rapidly the change will occur.

Human beings have both a larger thyroid than other animals, and a greater level of mental, emotional and physical activity. Thyroxin has a tremendous effect on the nerve cells in the adrenals glands and the ganglion cells throughout the sympathetic nervous system. This hormonal exertion increases short wave radiation, thereby charging the gray cells throughout the sympathetic system. We know that the nervous system controls the body. Since the thyroid exerts such influence over the nervous system and also regulates the short wave emanations given off by the body's cells, it follows that the thyroid is one of the chief governors of the body.

When the thyroid and adrenals are completely removed, the amount of short wave radiation is significantly reduced and the normal conscious state is depressed to the level of drowsiness, dullness and inertia. Without the adrenals, the thyroid loses its specific effect. In the case of thyroid removal, or loss of function, adrenaline loses the effect of increasing the conductivity and temperature of the brain, and concomitantly decreasing the conductivity and temperature of the other organs.

MORE ON THE ROLE OF THE THYROID HORMONE

Iodine metabolism and thyroid function are closely linked. Let me reiterate that thyroxin contains iodine in its most active, oxidized state. This condition has direct bearing on the hormone. Oxidization of iodine is critical to proper thyroxin functioning. Related chemicals, such as iodine, chlorine and bromine, referred to as halogens, are powerful oxidizing agents. This means that they are readily able to supply considerable energy for the enzyme reactions that occur in every cell of the body.

As we can determine from the preceding paragraph, the principle physiological function of the thyroid is to act as a catalyst for the oxidative reactions of the body. In fact, it controls the speed of these reactions. Let's think of the thyroid as a car's ignition system. If the timing of the ignition system is out of sync with the motor's revolutions, the car will not run smoothly. If the rate of ignition spark is slowed, the motor will also be slowed. On the other hand, if the rate of ignition spark is sped up, the motor runs faster. In the human body, thyroxin provides the spark for all oxidative processes. A car engine creates a perfect example: when thyroxin is abundant the car starts up quickly and responds efficiently to your commands. When thyroxin is scarce, oxidative processes are slowed. In other words, to compare with the car engine, if there is an abundance of thyroxin, these oxidative processes will be accelerated. When thyroxin is scarce, oxidative processes are slowed.

Thyroid abnormalities cause severe health problems. This is especially true if abnormalities are present during the early stages of development. A lack of thyroid gland development in young children results in a state known as cretinism. Cretinism can produce a whole host of difficulties, including low metabolic rate, low body temperature, obesity, slowed mental and physical development and a protruding abdomen. If the thyroid gland develops, but its activity is reduced a condition known as hypothyroidism occurs. Hypothyroidism, or underactive thyroid, can result in stunted growth, poor bone development, and changes in the texture of the skin.

Hyperthyroidism, or overactive thyroid, is often associated with a condition called goiter. Goiter, an enlargement of the thyroid gland itself, occurs in two ways. Simple, endemic goiter is usually caused by an inadequate supply of iodine in the diet, which results in low thyroxin levels. Low thyroxin levels create more TSH production by the pituitary gland. The thyroid is constantly stimulated, and thus becomes enlarged. Because of low blood thyroxin levels, the symptoms of simple goiter are not unlike those of hypothyroidism. Certain vegetables, such as turnips and rutabagas, have been known to cause thyroid enlargement. Upon digestion, these vegetables produce goitrins. Goitrins interfere with the pituitary-thyroid feedback and control mechanism. Fortunately today, thanks in large part to iodized table salt, hypothyroidism (due to iodine deficiency) is rare. The current epidemic of hypothyroidism has a less physical origin. Failure to speak your truth causes an energy stagnation. Eventually blood flow, cell regeneration and hormone function are blocked in the area, which sets the stage for thyroid deficiency. Most people with thyroid disease have pain in the neck muscles or spinal region.

The most common form of true hyperthyroidism, called Grave's disease, is associated with excessive levels of thyroxin in the blood (toxic goiter). The more obvious symptoms of true hyperthyroidism are nervousness, tiredness, weight loss and increased body temperature accompanied by sweating. With true hyperthyroidism, the entire metabolic process is sped up just as if we had sped up the motor in our car analogy.

In the case of hypothyroidism, the frustration built up in the throat as a result of not fully communicating one's needs and hopes, causes the body to allocate more energy to the thyroid and throat in an effort to get you to speak up. Common symptoms that accompany hypothyroidism are a bad temper and moodiness that get expressed in an angry way. These two diseases are two ends of the same spectrum.

There are a plethora of bodily functions and processes that are, in some way, controlled by the thyroid gland and its hormone, thyroxin. Certainly the liver, a vital organ which isolates and removes dangerous toxins from the body, is very much dependent on thyroxin. In fact, the liver is one of the largest users of thyroxin. Thyroxin is also important in that it plays a role in regulating the conversion and absorption of other chemicals so various tissues can use them. For example, iron is required for the synthesis of red blood cells; phosphate is incorporated into nerve and bone tissue, and is used extensively in the production of energy at the cellular level; and arsenic is regulated in connection with the keratin, a protein necessary to the structure of skin, hair and bones.

THE THYROID AND SPIRITUALITY

The thyroid gland is significant in that it controls the rapidity and intensity of exchange between subjective and objective consciousness. In other words, the thyroid helps us integrate what we feel with what we know. Development of the psychic attributes associated with the thyroid gland can be assisted by, among other things, the intonation of certain vowel sounds and the visualization of certain colors. For example, chanting THO (*prounounced zzzoh – found on the Healing Fire CD*) is known to stimulate the thyroid. When we consciously stimulate our glandular system, we allow the harmonious activity of the pineal, pituitary and thyroid to join forces with the harmonious influences of the spiritual centers to produce the appropriate atmosphere for mystical experience.

Just behind the thyroid gland in the neck are the united parathyroids, which function as a regulator of the flow of vibrations between the sympathetic and the cerebrospinal nervous systems. The parathyroid glands are four minute bodies lying just behind the thyroid. The parathyroid glands are exceptional because they ease pain and equalize the distribution of the psychic and physical vibrations of the human body, so as to establish a harmonic condition between them. Each of us generates energy from our mind/psyche and our body. These must be integrated for our total being to function well. The parathyroid glands are responsible for this. It is here where the first stages of Cosmic attunement begin, for through the functioning of the parathyroids the aura of the physical body is adjusted in its rates of vibration to be harmonious with the Cosmic rates of vibration. (The process of merging and quickening these two vibrations was an area of focus for the Rose Croix Kabbalists because of its crucial importance. The more efficient this is made through chanting and meditation, the more adept the spiritual student.)

A FINAL NOTE

Remember: never talk in order to conquer. One wrong word can open a wound that may never heal. When you bark at people instead of communicating harmoniously with them, you are "carving the brain." This means that you are attempting to imprint your views and opinions on another. This is molding, not communication. The one who uses words in the interest of victory has already been defeated. Communication builds tomorrow, not today, and yesterday has revealed your mistakes.

Those who communicate for the purpose of establishing a relationship consider the way the other person feels, what they are doing, where they are in their lives, what they want and how much they can handle. They relinquish themselves, their ego, to a sense of oneness with the other thereby creating a merger of security at a common frequency of communication. In this way, they are able to get at the other in a positive, healing and uplifting way. They are evolved beings with good in their hearts. They speak with the compassion of *we*, rather than the passion of *I*. Interestingly, true love permanently settles everything. It establishes the harmonious communication and care that may render actual words unnecessary. In other words, when two people experience true love, they create a living, inexplicable psyche and begin to speak through bodily vibrations. They simply know, feel and acknowledge the joys and pains of the other. Then, one kiss or one hug can say more than a thousand words.

CHAPTER TWELVE

Fire and Water

It has been established that humankind is a microcosm, which is an exact reflection of the macrocosm or universe. Therefore, all one has to do is observe nature to see how to behave in order to be happy and avoid needless suffering.

The male and female principles are the two forces that keep nature going. They are respectively known as *fire* and *water* or as *solar energy* and *lunar energy*. Happiness comes from a perfect balance of these two forces.

In a love relationship, the forces of fire and water are brought together. If one of the partners has a fiery temper, the other must have a cool or watery temper in order to balance the relationship. If both partners are hot-tempered, the relationship will inevitably end in failure. When fire meets fire, the heat produced sooner or later burns the relationship and separates the couple. The same is true for two people with cool or quiet dispositions. When both partners are quiet, the coolness increases and freezes the relationship, thereby creating extreme boredom, atrophy and depression. This too will eventually separate the couple.

Similarly, there cannot be two leaders. If the woman leads, the man must support in the leading strategy, and vice versa, for leading should be performed in the spirit of purest intention for the good of the family. It is not a control contest. In some couples the woman leads, whereas in others, it is the man. The one who either makes the majority of decisions or has the last word is considered the leader. The leader needs to remember that his or her electromagnetic field will determine the destiny of the family. When both lead, the relationship is in duality, which creates confusion and conflict. The force that bonds the relationship leaks, by virtue of not being whole. Only struggle, tension and separation meet the couple.

Leading should be performed from a place of oneness and mutual agreement, for in Oneness, the force is in its totality. Therefore, victory is the outcome. The couple moves their energy from duality to the Oneness of Divinity. The co-leader supports the leader. Certainly, it is neither a matter of chauvinism nor control. It is a matter of pure love, natural aptitude and support for the well-being of all involved.

The leader displays the fire energy, which is the driving force, while the co-leader is the water energy which directs the rate of expansion in the right direction. When both lead, it is difficult to control the expansion of fire because of the lack of water energy, and a crash is the most likely consequence. When no one leads, there is no movement forward, only stagnation and indecision.

The Sun is the symbol of the male principle and the Moon is the symbol of the female principle. As mentioned previously, the Moon is water and the Sun is fire. Seventy-five percent of the human body is made up of water. The Moon affects everything on Earth. It is the mother energy. Without women, there is no world, for the female energy rules the world. Women are the only reality. They are emotionally stronger and more intelligent than men. Although the woman is symbolically water, when she leads the couple she becomes the fire or expansion element in the couple. Fire constitutes the quality of leadership; it has nothing to do with their personal symbolic fire/Sun or water/Moon energies.

Women wax and wane like the Moon. All a man has to do is observe the Moon to know how to act with his mate. When a woman waxes, she is optimistic, positive and outgoing, and she needs the closeness of her partner. If he is not there, he runs the risk of being eclipsed. When she wanes, she needs her space to regroup, so it is best that her partner respect her space.

A man has two choices when he deals with a woman. First, he can choose to behave like the Sun, meaning that he can be centered and steady as she waxes and wanes. This is the wisest and safest way. His other choice is to wax and wane with her, but he must be in synchronicity with her cycles. In other words, if the woman waxes, then the man must wax. If she wanes, he must also wane. If she waxes and he wanes instead of waxing with her, trouble is near. If he waxes while she wanes, the couple is definitely headed for trouble.

THE TREE OF LIFE

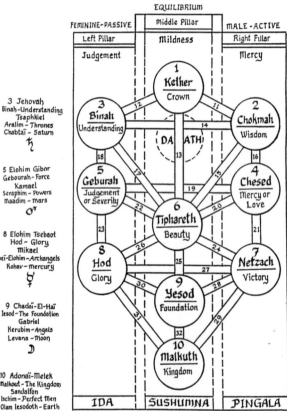

1 Ehieh
Kether- The Crown
Metatron
Hayot Ha-Kodesch - Seraphs
Reschit Ha-Galgalim - The first vortex (Neptune)

EQUILIBRIUM

FEMININE - PASSIVE   middle Pillar   MALE - ACTIVE

Left Pillar   Mildness   Right Pillar

Judgement   Mercy

1 Kether Crown

3 Binah Understanding

2 Chokmah Wisdom

DAATH

5 Geburah — Judgement or Severity

4 Chesed — Mercy or Love

6 Tiphareth Beauty

8 Hod Glory

7 Netzach Victory

9 Yesod Foundation

10 Malkuth Kingdom

IDA   SUSHUMNA   PINGALA

3 Jehovah
Binah - Understanding
Tsaphkiel
Aralim - Thrones
Chabtaï - Saturn

5 Elohim Gibor
Gebourah - Force
Kamael
Seraphim - Powers
Maadim - Mars

8 Elohim Tsebaot
Hod - Glory
Mikael
Bneï-Elohim - Archangels
Kohav - mercury

9 Chadaï - El - Haï
Iesod - The Foundation
Gabriel
Kerubim - Angels
Levana - moon

10 Adonaï - Melek
Malkout - The Kingdom
Sandalfon
Ischim - Perfect men
Olam Iesodoth - Earth

2 Iah
Hokmah - Wisdom
Raziel
Ophanim - Cherubim
Mazaloth - The Zodiac (Uranus)

4 El
Hesed - Mercy
Tsadkiel
Hachmalim - Dominations
Tsedek - Jupiter

7 Jehovah Tsebaot
Netzach - Victory
Haniel
Elohim - Principalities
Noga - Venus

6 Eloha ve Daath
Tipheret - Beauty
Raphaël
Malahim - Virtues
Chemesch - Sun

CHAPTER THIRTEEN

Kabbalah and Relationships

Kabbalah, which means "receiving," is an ancient and powerful science for spiritual growth and understanding one's self in relation to the Universe. In the past, the wisdom of Kabbalah was available only to a select few. As we enter the Age of Aquarius, or the Age of Light, this knowledge is essential for living a full and complete life, complementing all aspects of the self and spirit. Kabbalah gives you access to the power and knowledge of the higher worlds. These ancient teachings form the foundation in which you can excel and transform your life, your relationships, your life's work, your fears, your addictions, and the very core of your being.

What is the divine wisdom referred to as Kabbalah? It is the art of receiving light, and light is the principle of fulfillment. Unhappiness and suffering come from darkness, and darkness is the absence of light. For humans to be happy, they must have light, for where there is light, one cannot find darkness.

King Solomon was one of the wisemen who enormously contributed to the wisdom of Kabbalah. In the book of wisdom of King Solomon included in the Apocrypha, Solomon says, "For God Himself gave me an unerring knowledge of the things that are, to know the constitution of the world, the beginning and the end and middle of time, the alteration of the solstices, the change of the seasons and the positions of the planets, the nature of living creatures, and the thoughts of men, all things that are either secret or manifest I learned. For He that is the artificer of all things taught me this wisdom."

How did this come about? If you continue to look further in the first book of Kings, Chapter 3, you will read that God appeared to Solomon in a dream at night and said, "Ask something of me and I will give it to you."

Solomon answered, "O Lord, my God, you have made me your servant, King to succeed my father David; but I am a mere youth, not knowing at all how to act. I serve you in the midst of the people whom you have chosen, a people so vast that it cannot be numbered or counted. Give your servant, therefore, an understanding heart to judge your people and to distinguish right from wrong. For who is able to govern this vast people of yours?" Solomon made this request.

So God said to him, "Because you have asked for this, not for a long life for yourself, nor for riches, nor for the life of your enemies, but for understanding so that you may know what is right, I do as you requested. I give you a heart so wise and understanding that there has never been anyone like you up to now, and after you there will come no one to equal you."

King Solomon is the only person who received the fullness of the divine spiritual wisdom known as the Kabbalah. He then passed this wisdom to the workers who helped him build the temple of Jerusalem in order to remind humankind of their origin and their destiny. Upon completion of this house of God, and through the advice of some of his collaborators, he rose to the highest degree of his glory. Bedazzled by the splendors of his throne, he eventually lost sight of the wisdom. This caused some of his closest supporters to desert him, and thus take this knowledge and spread it to other lands.

Kabbalah is a subject so vast that volumes have been written about it. For the purposes of this book, I will focus on the practical aspects of Kabbalah as it pertains to relationships.

The Seven Archangels

The basis of the holy Kabbalah is the sacred Tree of Life, which consists of ten spheres joined by 22 lines. The ten spheres, known as Sephiroth or the emanations of life, are basically a Gnostic diagram. These spheres correspond to different levels of our mental, spiritual and physical life. Each sphere on the Tree of Life also corresponds to one of the planetary bodies. In order, we have Neptune, Uranus, Saturn, Jupiter, Mars, Sun, Venus, Mercury, Moon and Earth. Each of these spheres/planets has an archangel who is in charge of the angels of that particular area. They are respectively governed by the archangels *Metatron, Raziel, Tsaphkiel, Tsadkiel, Kamael, Raphael, Hanael, Michael, Gabriel,* and *Sandalfon.*

Regarding the function of the seven main archangels and what they give when called upon:

Tsaphkiel of Saturn bestows blessings of knowledge and understanding.

Tsadkiel of Jupiter brings good fortune.

Kamael of Mars gives divine protection from all aggression.

Raphael of the Sun gives health and wealth.

Hanael of Venus bestows love and happiness.

Michael of Mercury gives success and intelligence.

Gabriel of the Moon gives peace and harmony.

Since this is a book about love, it is very important to work with Venus—the planet of love and beauty. It also rules Friday. Everything you buy on Friday will radiate the love and beauty of Venus. To enhance the energy of Venus, purchase flowers, jewelry, clothes or gifts for your partner on this day. The response will be extremely positive. You will notice that people always love what you buy on Friday. Also, choose this day to work on personal beauty, such as getting your hair styled.

Another way to work with Venus is to call upon the archangel, *Hanael.* Suppose that you either have a problem with your love mate or desire to enhance your relationship. There are various procedures to get in touch with the angels. Here is one of them:

- Light a candle, for its light will remind you of the presence of God. Wash your hands and drink a glass of water to purify yourself. Take a few deep breaths to quiet the mind before you proceed.
- First, invoke the blessings of the archangel **Metatron**, chief of all the archangels, by vibrating his name 3 times.
- Secondly, invoke the protective light of the archangel **Raziel** by vibrating his name 3 times.
- Thirdly, invoke the support of **Sandalphon**, the archangel responsible for the Earth, 3 times.
- Finally, invoke the archangel in charge of your particular case. In this instance, call upon **Hanael**, the archangel of Venus, 3 times and request assistance for your relationship.

The divine spiritual wisdom, or Kabbalah, is the key to the mysteries of the creation of time, space and humanity. Astrology and numerology have always been used for guidance and compatibility, but the fact remains that the twelve signs of astrology originate from the seven creative planets governed by the seven Archangels who sit before the throne of God. Based upon the numeric pattern of creation of 3 − 7 − 12, the number seven is above twelve. Therefore, those seven planets show you in a practical manner how the unseen forces of nature move in your life in relationship to the universe. The pattern of seven follows the seal of King Solomon, to whom God gave the perfect understanding of the secrets of nature. This seal demonstrates the movement of the unseen forces of nature.

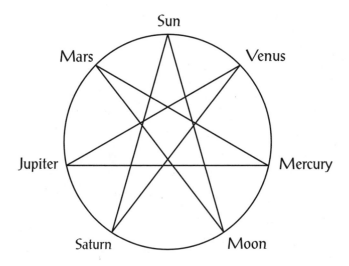

Seal of Solomon

Every human being has a vibration and his or her life has a particular rhythm. Certain segments of the rhythms are ruled by particular forces symbolized by the planets. The names that we give to the planets are a way to identify the forces behind these rhythms. Whether we know it or not, human life is strongly influenced by these rhythms.

When to Enter a Relationship

The principles I am now about to pass on, I have found to be the most accurate, as well as extremely helpful. I feel sure that knowledge of this truth will be of the greatest practical utility to every man or woman desiring to build, nurture and maintain a healthy love relationship. These truths, which have never before been made public, are the unseen forces that direct every relationship. Ignorance of these laws is the disease which continues to brutally shorten the lives of many relationships and, in a bitter way, break the hearts of love partners. Therefore, it is vital for love partners to take the time to see which way the powerful forces of nature are moving. Knowing the implications and applications of these forces, coupled with personal responsibility, will give any man or woman a repertoire of expanded options in his or her actions regarding one's love life. I could write an entire volume on these laws, but in the following necessarily condensed chapter, you will find the general law explained to sufficiently elucidate this system.

WORKING WITH THE PHASES OF THE MOON

Every person needs to seek assistance from the moon for any successful endeavor. Consider the moon in all your daily affairs. The ups and downs of life are symbolized by the waxing and waning of the moon. During the waxing moon, the energy of the body moves into our angelic part, bringing out the light in us. Light is the principle of fulfillment, therefore, the rising moon, which is the waxing period, is used to bring things into one's life or to accelerate the growth of any project. It is the best time to start a relationship, get married, or start a new job or project.

During the waning moon, the energy of the human body moves into our animal part, bringing out the darkness in us. Problems may arise from darkness. Entering a relationship while the moon is waning will not prove beneficent. This period, from the full moon to the day before the new moon, is the best time to remove things from your life, not start something. Actually, it is the best time for divorce. Do not use the time dedicated to taking things out of one's life to bring new things in! By doing so, you are increasing the probability of failure. This failure may be minimized by the impact of a more favorable period—it is your choice! Keep in mind that the waxing moon is the period between the new moon and the day before the

full moon, whereas the waning moon is from the full moon to the day before the new moon.

LAW OF THE SEVEN CREATIVE PLANETS

Nature, in all her mysterious dealings with life, uses the mystical number seven, which is recognized as a number of divine power. From the earliest days of the world's history up to our time, the number seven has played a most important part in every aspect of the world. This is reflected in the seven days of the week that we find in every continent, country, race and culture. Also, it is known that the entire human body undergoes a complete change every seven years. This mysterious number corresponds to the seven Archangels of the lord whose magnetic influence operates through the seven planets and radiates all over the earth. In relation to the number seven, there are spiritual facts about love relationships completely unknown to many.

There is a law known as the Law of the Seven Creative Planets. The matrix of change we call nature is structured by its forces. From the womb to the grave we are governed by its influences. Your day of birth sets this clock in motion, and every relationship dances with these planets as partners. The understanding and application of the seven creative planets can become a source of infinite wisdom, particularly your personal yearly cycle. This cycle, which is an energy flow available for everyone, is there to protect you by taking away your downfalls and showing your pitfalls. Happiness and love is achieved by working with your personal cycle. It shows you very clearly the most auspicious time to enter a relationship or get married for a more harmonious and fulfilling love life. Here is how you can determine your energy flow or personal yearly cycle.

The year is divided into seven periods of 52 days. Each period is ruled by one of the seven planets—Sun, Moon, Mars, Mercury, Jupiter, Venus and Saturn. Each of the seven creative planets has a direct impact on your yearly cycle. Your personal year begins with your day of birth and continues to the day before your next birthday. Suppose you were born on March 21—your new year would begin on this day. For example, the planetary cycle of someone born on March 21 follows the schematic on the next page.

Planetary Cycle/The Seven Periods

EXAMPLE: MARCH 21 BIRTHDATE

SUN	March 21–May 11
MOON	May 12–July 2
MARS	July 3–August 23
MERCURY	August 24–October 14
JUPITER	October 15–December 5
VENUS	December 6–January 26
SATURN	January 27–March 20

The Seven Periods

Our world is comprised of pairs. Therefore, life is engendered through the forces of vibration. This vibration of life presents itself in many ways. Day and night, good and evil, male and female are some of these ways. Within your own cycle's influence these planets represent your "best" and "worst" time for specific accomplishments. For example, the Sun, Jupiter and Venus tend to be beneficent planets, whereas Mars and Saturn tend toward challenging aspects. The Moon and Mercury have a more neutral countenance.

The clock of the seven planets is placed in motion with the bonding of a relationship. The sexual act, or bonding, determines the first day of the relationship. If the relationship makes it to marriage, then the marriage date overrides the previous starting date. In other words, the marriage date becomes the new date for the impact of the influence of the seven creative planets.

Sun Period

The Sun is ruled by the Lord of Light. Light is the principle of fulfillment. It preserves your reputation. This period is extremely auspicious for starting a relationship or getting married. Above all, entering a relationship during this period while the Moon is waxing is excellent. By doing so, you are giving the relationship all the

chances it needs to survive any trial, and your married life becomes more peaceful and harmonious. The Sun period promises success for your plans. This is a period when the Universe gives you the green light to do practically anything and be who you want to be. It provides you with an abundance of new energy. This is the best time for initiation, growth and expansion. You can improve your reputation, start or accomplish anything you want, and many opportunities will come to you. All the obstacles that may have prevented you from having what you want will easily be overcome. If you realize that you have complications because you married at the wrong time, you can remarry now to cool things down. Since it is unusual for both partners to be in their Sun period, it is preferable that the one leading the couple be in his/her fortunate period. That's because the electromagnetic field of the leader affects the destiny of the couple.

Suggested mantra meditation: Lumen de Lumine; RaMaDaSa; Mystic Light CD (#1–RaMa Ram Ram, #3); Heaven's Touch CD (#1–Guru Ram Das); Greenhouse CD (#1–Har Gobinday, #2–Har Haray Haree, #3–Ad Such); Blissful Spirit CD (#2) or Sounds of the Ether CD (#1).

Moon Period

The Moon is ruled by the Lord of Sensitivity. You can enter a relationship in the Moon period, but make sure it is when the moon is waxing. New relationships can be problematic during this period while the moon is waning. During the waning moon this planet becomes like Mars or Saturn. Therefore, do not enter a relationship or marriage at this time. The Moon influences everything on Earth, for her vibrations are felt from the tides of the ocean to the waves of the human mind. The Moon represents fluctuation. You may hesitate or vacillate in decisions. If you find it difficult to make up your mind, wait for the next period. Your affairs may move slowly during the Moon period. You should be diplomatic and avoid arguments. In other words, be cool. This is a time to work with others, to observe and listen. Realize that if you do, the change is not long-term. This is the best time for short trips. It is a good time to deal with the public. Men will get along better with women than with other men. The time of the waxing moon during one's Moon period is a good time for marriage proposals.

Suggested mantra meditation: RaMaDaSa; *Heaven's Touch CD (#2–Sat Narayan); Soul Trance CD (#1–Wahe Guru Wahe Jio);* or *Blissful Spirit CD (#1–Wahe Guru Wahe Jio, #2–Ganputi Mantra).*

Mars Period

Mars is ruled by the Lord of War. Avoid entering a relationship during this period. Mars and Saturn are challenging planets, and the 52 days that each of these planets rule are accident-prone times of trial. One can make all types of mistakes that will resurface karmically later. Therefore, neither enter a relationship nor get married during these periods. In addition, it is an especially poor time when the moon is waning, as any relationship or marriage entered during this period will sooner or later end with serious complications and possibly painful divorce. However, if one enters a relationship in such a period and makes it to marriage, the negative energy can be deflected by setting the marriage date during one's Sun, Jupiter or Venus periods, especially while the moon is waxing. If you happened to get married during your Mars or Saturn periods and are undergoing marital problems, you can remarry your partner during your best period to cool things down.

This period will put a lot of physical energy and "fire" at your disposal. Use this energy wisely and refrain from being impulsive. Use critical judgment in this time, avoid anger and speak politely. Drive carefully and take good care of your health. By choosing the right time, place and date, you can resolve any confrontation. Feel empowered and be the one who makes the rules. You can take advantage of the Mars energy to improve your health and remove obstacles from your life. Refrain from excess sexual activities. You may be tempted to do projects that will not benefit you. For women, it is the best period to ask men for anything. This is not a good time to start a relationship.

Suggested mantra meditation: Triple Mantra or *Heaven's Touch CD (#1–Guru Ram Das, #2–Sat Narayan).*

Mercury Period

Mercury is ruled by the Lord of Communication. You can enter a relationship in the Mercury period, but make sure it is when the moon is waxing. New relationships can be problematic during this period while the moon is waning. During the waning moon this planet becomes like Mars or Saturn. Therefore, do not enter a relationship or marriage at this time. During the Mercury period, you will experience a lot of changes. It may feel as if you are in a battlefield, where the only thing you have for guidance is your intuition. Your intuitive intelligence should be used to the utmost. During this time, mental and spiritual bodies are stimulated. It is the best time to put your ideas to work, write books, study, collect information and make plans. This is the best time to deal with children or for a woman to conceive. Go with the flow, but be very discriminating. Do not leave your personal belongings unattended.

Suggested mantra meditation: Green House CD (#2–Har Haray Haree Wahe Guru); Soul Trance CD (#3–SaReGaMa); or Mystic Light CD (#4–Har Haray Haree).

Jupiter Period

Jupiter is ruled by the Lord of Material and Spiritual Richness. This is a very favorable time for starting a relationship or getting married. Above all, entering a relationship during this period while the Moon is waxing is excellent. By doing so, you are giving the relationship all the chances it needs to survive any trial, and your married life becomes more peaceful and harmonious. If after reading this book, you realize that you have complications because you married at the wrong time, you can remarry now to cool things down. Since it is unusual for both partners to be in this period, it is preferable that the one leading the couple be in his/her fortunate period. That's because the electromagnetic field of the leader affects the destiny of the couple. Jupiter is the planet of material and spiritual abundance. This is the time when the Lord of Prosperity will easily smile upon you. Take this time to prosper and expand. Be ambitious and take risks, such as buying stocks. During this period, resolve matters of the law.

It is a good time to deal with lawyers, judges, government officials and people of wealth. You may easily gain popularity in this period.

Suggested mantra meditation: Lumen de Lumine; RaMaDaSa; Mystic Light CD (#1, #3); Heaven's Touch CD (Guru Ram Das); Greenhouse CD (#1, #2); or Blissful Spirit CD (#2).

Venus Period

Venus is the Lord of Love. This period is extremely auspicious for starting a relationship or getting married. Above all, entering a relationship during this period while the Moon is waxing is excellent. By doing so, you are giving the relationship all the chances it needs to survive any trial, and your married life becomes more peaceful and harmonious. If after reading this book, you realize that you have complications because you married at the wrong time, you can remarry now to cool things down. Since it is unusual for both partners to be in this period, it is preferable that the one leading the couple be in his/her fortunate period. That's because the electromagnetic field of the leader affects the destiny of the couple. The Venus period is a time for rest, play and fun. Loosen up. It is an excellent time to get involved with music, art and dance. You should now take good care of yourself and treat yourself right. It is the best time for taking long or short trips, improving relationships and making friends. Men can ask women for anything. This is a good time to buy all your clothes and jewelry. Just remember, this is an excellent time to fall in love or propose marriage.

Suggested mantra meditation: Lumen de Lumine; RaMaDaSa; Sounds of the Ether CD (#4–Hari Har); Mystic Light CD (#1, #3); Heaven's Touch CD (Guru Ram Das); Greenhouse CD (#1, #2);or Blissful Spirit CD (#2).

Saturn Period

Saturn is ruled by the Lord of Karma. Avoid entering a relationship during this period. Saturn and Mars are challenging planets, and the 52 days that each of these planets rule are accident-prone times of trial. One can make all types of mistakes that will resurface karmically later. Therefore, neither enter a relationship nor get married during those periods. In addition, it is an especially bad time when the moon is waning (between the full moon and the day before the new moon), as any relationship or marriage entered during that time will sooner or later end with serious complications and possibly painful divorce. However, if one enters a relationship in such a period and makes it to marriage, the negative energy can possibly be deflected by setting the marriage date during one's Sun, Jupiter or Venus periods, especially while the moon is waxing. If you happened to get married during your Mars or Saturn periods and are undergoing marital problems, you can remarry in your best period to cool things down.

During the Saturn period, take time to meditate and further your spiritual development. You may be tempted to take foolish actions and make poor decisions. Avoid scandal and gossip. You may feel confined and restricted in this period. Use this period to look within and study both yourself and your surroundings. Do not miss meditation, and do not let a day go by without strengthening your aura. Get rid of anything you do not need. Try to understand the unseen forces that direct our lives. Spend a lot of time reading spiritual and inspirational books. The best way to think of Saturn is like the night before the day. At night, everything slows down. It is a time to rest and revitalize the body. Progress is slow and arduous. In fact, you may be under the impression that nothing works the way you want it to. Remember, Saturn represents patience and discipline. It would be in your best interest to rest, organize, plan, and gather your resources.

Suggested mantra meditation: Lumen de Lumine; Triple Mantra; Sounds of the Ether CD (#1–Ad Such); or Heaven's Touch CD (#1–Guru Ram Das, #2–Sat Narayan).

Additional meditations for each period can be found in *Lifting the Veil.*

The Karmic Wheel or Consciousness Cycle

Just imagine how you would feel if you were thrown into a fight with someone or something you could not see. What would your chances of winning be? Realistically, you and I know that it is extremely difficult, if not impossible, to fight anything you cannot see and still win. That is certainly the reason why we were blessed with intuition: in order to see the unseen and protect ourselves. Without the salvation of intuition, complete tragedy would befall humankind. We would surely be like speeding cars without drivers, and a crash would definitely be the end result. Therefore, it is crucial to take the time to see which way the powerful forces of nature are moving. This knowledge will give you early warnings of pitfalls, so that you may save your love life from unnecessary troubles.

Before proceeding with the consciousness cycle, I would like to describe here what happens within the first 12 months of a relationship. The first day of a relationship is determined by the actual first mutual act of sexual bonding. This is the "birthday" of the relationship, which is influenced by the particular planet that it shares.

There are challenging phases that an intimate couple must overcome for a relationship to endure.

The first four months of a relationship are vital in establishing a solid foundation. If a foundation is weak, the structure always collapses at the first trial.

The first 52 days which follow mutual bonding are governed by the Sun. This explains the intensity of passion, emotion, fun and excitement that couples usually experience in their beginning period.

Then come the next 52 days, ruled by the Moon period. The Moon signifies fluctuation. It either pulls you apart or brings you closer. In the worst-case scenario, the Moon pulls you apart and Mars severs the relationship. It is for this reason that some relationships end between the third and fourth months. In the best-case scenario the Moon brings you closer and Mars strengthens the relationship, thus allowing it to go beyond the fourth month.

Sometimes a challenge is felt early in the eight month, before the couple reaches the Saturn period of the first yearly cycle.

REGARDING THE KARMIC WHEEL OR CONSCIOUSNESS CYCLE

There are spiritual facts about love relationships completely unknown to many. One important fact indicates that every love relationship has an invisible soul, which goes through a karmic wheel or consciousness cycle of seven years.

It is the first sexual act or marriage date that puts the clock of the karmic wheel in motion. Those seven years are respectively ruled by the planetary bodies through which the seven archangels before the throne of God work. The order of those planets are as follows: Sun, Moon, Mars, Mercury, Jupiter, Venus and Saturn. Therefore, from the Sun (first year), the soul of the love relationship proceeds to the Moon (second year), then to Mars (third year), from Mars to Mercury (fourth year), Mercury to Jupiter (fifth year), Jupiter to Venus (sixth year), and Venus to Saturn (seventh year) ending one complete consciousness cycle. If the love bond is healthy and strong enough to survive the challenges of time and space presented by the first karmic wheel, it then proceeds to the next karmic wheel. In the case of a 49-year-old marriage or healthy love relationship, we have a clear example of seven karmic wheels or consciousness cycles of seven years each. Those seven cycles are similarly ruled by the Sun, Moon, Mars, Mercury, Jupiter, Venus and Saturn. The love relationship starts with the Sun cycle of seven years and proceeds to the Moon cycle, from that to the Mars cycle, from Mars to the Mercury cycle, Mercury to the Jupiter cycle, Jupiter to Venus cycle, and Venus to the Saturn cycle, which completes the last seven years. If the marriage survives the first seven cycles, or 49 years, it goes on to the next group of cycles until either divorce or death stops the process.

REGARDING THE INFLUENCE OF THE SEVEN
PLANETS ON THE YEARS

The magnetic influence of the Archangels operates through the aforementioned seven creative planets and radiates all over the earth. The planets that compose the karmic wheel are the universal laws in charge of the regularity and order of everything in heaven and on earth. They make sure that we fit in with the natural laws, system and order of things to which we owe our being.

There are a few enlightening things in matters relating to the consciousness cycle of a love relationship that I have found not only helpful, but also extremely reliable. I am sure that you have heard the saying, "The Seven Year Itch," meaning that the seventh year is the most difficult in a marriage or intimate relationship. It is invariably conceded by most long-term married couples that the seventh year of a relationship is the most difficult, but to this day, no one I know was ever able to explain why. The reason is simple. The years ruled by the Sun, Jupiter and Venus are favorable, whereas the Moon and Mercury years can go either way. The third and seventh years are the most challenging, because they are respectively ruled by Mars and Saturn. Mars is the Lord of War and Saturn the Lord of Karma; their role is to create karmic balance. Of these two challenging planets, Saturn is the primary one. This is why most people find the seventh year of a love relationship very challenging. This also explains why many relationships end after the sixth year. The other truth not to be ignored is that a great number of love relationships cannot even make it past the third or Mars year. Any marriage or first sexual act performed at the wrong time, or any relationship entered impulsively, no matter how beautiful things may seem, will find it extremely difficult to make it past the third or seventh years. This is because people have been unable to recognize the laws of nature as applied to love relationships. Therefore, they knowingly or unknowingly misuse their free will in ignoring the sacredness of love relationships, as well as the respect and commitment involved. Thus they continue to damage themselves and others, increasing the number of broken hearts. This is why divine justice operates through the seven planets and uses the karmic wheel to restore order and harmony in all things. Just remember, the seven planets are both the police and the laws of the universe.

The first year, known as the Sun year, is usually fun. This explains the intensity of passion, emotion and excitement that couples usually experience in the first year. Love is good, because the sun is shining on the love relationship. During the Sun year, we usually do not find fault with our love mate; he or she is perfect.

Then comes the second year, or the Moon year. The Moon stands for duality, fluctuation and sensitivity. The Moon either pulls you apart or brings you closer. We start to become sensitive about some of the things our partner does. In the worst-case scenario, the Moon year pulls you apart and the Mars year severs the relationship. It is for this reason that some relationships end between the second and third years. In the best-case scenario, the Moon year brings you closer and the Mars year strengthens the relationship, thus allowing it to proceed to the seventh year.

In the third or Mars year, we start to become reactive. Mars stands for impatience, aggression and impulsive behavior. The behavior of our partner that did not bother us in the Sun year starts to get on our nerves in the Mars year. We lose patience and become less tolerant. Each partner must control impulsive behavior, otherwise he or she may be led to do something foolish that often ends the relationship. You must be strong to be able to withstand any temptations which may come your way and recognize them for what they are. Every temptation overcome gives you a deeper inner-strength and stability, making you able to face anything without wavering.

Next comes the Mercury year, or fourth year. You must take the time to really communicate with your partner. Take time to travel and relax together.

During the fifth year, or Jupiter year, focus on opportunities to expand and prosper together. Also, arrange to go out for fine dining.

The Venus year, or sixth year, is a time to really take care of yourself and look more beautiful than usual. Venus stands for love, beauty and fun. If you have forgotten how to be romantic, here is your chance to make up for it. Be really loving and offer flowers to your partner. By being kind and caring, you give the relationship the strength that it needs to survive the following year.

Then comes the seventh year, ruled by Saturn—the Lord of karma. This is usually a very challenging time full of tests. Sometimes a challenge is felt as early as the sixth year. During your Saturn year, all the karmic lessons about the relationship that you have been running away from will come back to seek balance. This is a time where some of the destructive habits of the relationship must be replaced by healthy ones in order to move forward. Saturn reveals in a hard way what is not working in your love relationship and where you need to change. This process often brings disturbances to the mind, body and spirit, making you lonely and frustrated. Saturn is confining and limiting. It can bring humiliation, delays, obstacles and problems with the law. This is a time for you to sharpen your listening skills. Meditation and prayer are your best tools. As one mystic said, prayer is an ineffable act because it does not claim to be anything, yet it can do everything. Prayer transforms all misfortunes into delights, because it is the daughter of love. This will help make this time easier for you.

Sun Consciousness Cycle

The Sun stands for expansion and growth.

AGE OF THE RELATIONSHIP

0–1	Sun	Joyful.
1–2	Moon	Fluctuation and sensitivity. Emotions and indecision.
2–3	Mars	First major challenge.
3–4	Mercury	Communication is essential.
4–5	Jupiter	Spirituality is needed.
5–6	Venus	Renew romance.
6–7	Saturn	Second major challenge. Limitation.

Moon Consciousness Cycle

Fluctuation and sensitivity. True personality is revealed.

AGE OF THE RELATIONSHIP

7–8	Sun	Relatively joyful.
8–9	Moon	Fluctuation and sensitivity. Emotions and indecision.
9–10	Mars	Challenge. This will bring out your anger.
10–11	Mercury	Communication is essential.
11–12	Jupiter	Spirituality is needed.
12–13	Venus	Renew romance.
13–14	Saturn	Challenge. Restriction. This brings out your fears.

Mars Consciousness Cycle

Love undergoes a challenging time. Any superficial union will never pass this point. The rose glasses come off; truth is revealed.

AGE OF THE RELATIONSHIP

14–15	Sun	Not always so joyful.
15–16	Moon	Fluctuation and sensitivity. Emotions and indecision.
16–17	Mars	Aggressively challenging.
17–18	Mercury	Communication is essential.
18–19	Jupiter	Spirituality is needed.
19–20	Venus	Renew romance.
20–21	Saturn	Deviously challenging and restricting. The night before the day.

Mercury Consciousness Cycle

Honest communication is a must. Adaptibility, flexibility and understanding.

AGE OF THE RELATIONSHIP

21–22	Sun	Relatively joyful.
22–23	Moon	Fluctuation and sensitivity. Emotions and indecision.
23–24	Mars	Challenge.
24–25	Mercury	Communication is essential.
25–26	Jupiter	Spirituality is needed.
26–27	Venus	Renew romance.
27–28	Saturn	Challenge. Restriction.

Jupiter Consciousness Cycle

Spirituality and expansion.

AGE OF THE RELATIONSHIP

28–29	Sun	Joyful.
29–30	Moon	Fluctuation and sensitivity. Emotions and indecision.

30–31	Mars	Somewhat challenging.
31–32	Mercury	Communication is essential.
32–33	Jupiter	Spirituality is needed. Very expansive, prosperous year.
33–34	Venus	Renew romance.
34–35	Saturn	Somewhat challenging. Restriction.

Venus Consciousness Cycle

Renew romance and love.

AGE OF THE RELATIONSHIP

35–36	Sun	Joyful.
36–37	Moon	Fluctuation and sensitivity. Emotions and indecision.
37–38	Mars	Somewhat challenging.
38–39	Mercury	Communication is essential.
39–40	Jupiter	Spirituality is needed.
40–41	Venus	Renew romance.
41–42	Saturn	Somewhat challenging. Restriction.

Saturn Consciousness Cycle

The strength of the relationship is tested. A strong spiritual base is needed to overcome this challenge.

AGE OF THE RELATIONSHIP

42–43	Sun	Not always joyful.
43–44	Moon	Fluctuation and sensitivity. Emotions and indecision.
44–45	Mars	Very challenging.
45–46	Mercury	Communication is essential.
46–47	Jupiter	Spirituality is needed.
47–48	Venus	Renew romance.
48–49	Saturn	Very challenging. Restriction.

CHAPTER FOURTEEN

The Predominating Vibration
of a Relationship

My experience with counseling over thirty-two thousand people and diligently recording my observations, including the many years of teaching, traveling and meeting some of the world's best healers, has allowed me to derive a very accurate system that reveals some of the unseen forces which influence partners in a relationship. In this book, we will only focus on the day of birth—something easily learned about someone you might want to date. (Sometimes people are sensitive about revealing their age through their year of birth, but in this system you don't need to know that.) Once you know the day of birth, you can use it to determine the energy ruling the relationship through the 22 major arcana of the tarot.

The tarot is a system of complex symbology that comes from the *Rota*, which signifies the Wheel of the Torah—the esoteric Hebrew name for the law. According to the teachings, Moses studied under Yothora, who was a great Kabbalist, for 40 years. After his initiation, Yothora gave his daughter Ziporah to Moses to marry. Ziporah means Sephirah. Then he left the house in order to go and deliver the Jews from the Egyptians. It is important to remember that by working with the tarot keys we are actually consulting the Torah. In other words, the tarot is the key to the Torah. The essence of the Zohar is contained in the various symbols of the tarot.

Now, let's go back to the numbers. By determining the number of your relationship you can find out its root vibration and fate. The number of any relationship is the combined birthdays of each of its partners. In practical Kabbalah, the day of birth is full of information. When the birth dates of two people are added together, that number is key in revealing the strengths and weaknesses of that particular relationship. Why? Because the numerical value of the combined birthdays is associated with the 22 letters of the Hebrew alphabet. And those 22 letters relate to the 22 major Arcana of the tarot, which come from the Rota, or Wheel of the Torah. Once you know the tarot card that symbolizes your relationship, then you can find out which planet rules the relationship. By knowing the planet, you can figure out the astrological signs that govern the relationship. With all this information, you can create the joyful relationship you want. In addition, any challenges the two of you face can easily be overcome by merging with the laws of the universe and constructively transmuting your negative patterns, thereby inviting the inflow and outflow of God's bounty into your love life. In summary, the number derived from your combined birthdays is the soul of your relationship.

To find the ruling energies behind a relationship, take the day of birth of each person and add them together. All birthdays from 1 to 11 *should not* be reduced before adding, whereas all birthdays above 11 *should* be reduced once prior to adding them together. The number you get corresponds to a particular tarot card, which represents the energy ruling the relationship. To find out the planet ruling the relationship, you reduce the relationship number to a single number. Then finally, you determine the zodiac sign of the relationship from its planet. For example, let's take a couple where one person's birthday is January 11 (which should not be reduced) and the other's birthday is August 26 (which reduces to 8: $2 + 6 = 8$). 11 added to 8 equals 19. Look up the tarot card 19, which turns out to be the card that symbolizes The Sun. To find the planet, you reduce the number to a single digit. In our example 19 would become 1, which in practical numerology also relates to the Sun. The astrological signs governing the relationship are derived from the planet. In our example, the Sun rules the zodiac sign of Leo.

This system offers partners the ability to constructively transmute their negative patterns and bring out all the joyful, healthy aspects of their ruling energies.

0/22 — THE FOOL

The beginning/the end. Trust, courageous leaps and creativity. Trust the voice of the heart. Be careful of delusion. Blind presumption; success followed by loss; entrapment; willful injury; folly; false judgment owing to the influence of others. Eccentricity. Idealism. This is not a very good energy for material things. Wrong doings; possible failure. Be careful of illness.

INFLUENCE ON RELATIONSHIP
This relationship cannot survive without trust. Honesty is important. Communication between both partners must be clear and direct. Practice good listening skills. Do not assume anything. Avoid blind presumption and be cautious of delusion. Lighten your demands on your partner. Treat your partner with kindness and consideration. Examine your own faults.

PLANETARY INFLUENCE
A relationship with this vibration is ruled by Uranus. This relationship would benefit from open and honest communication. Practice listening and avoid being too outspoken.

ASTROLOGICAL INFLUENCE
Although 4 is ruled by Uranus, in practical numerology, it is associated with the number 1. The number 1 is the positive aspect of the Sun on the physical plane, whereas 4 is the negative aspect of the Sun on the spiritual plane. The corresponding zodiac sign of the Sun is Leo. Therefore, you need to be loving, optimistic, and have integrity. Avoid egotism, and don't be too forceful or temperamental.

1 — THE MAGICIAN

Initiative; creative will; invention; construction; skill; wisdom; mysteries; adaptation. Sometimes occult wisdom. All forms of communication and creative potential. Practical realization; male principle; new enterprise.

INFLUENCE ON RELATIONSHIP
Do not be too critical or judgmental. Be aware of your partner's feelings. In this relationship you must learn to serve your partner. Through giving, you heal your fears and allow the universe to support the union. Make sure you do not cut yourself off from your partner.

PLANETARY INFLUENCE
A relationship with this vibration is ruled by the Sun, therefore it is best to bring in the qualities of the Sun. This relationship would benefit from sharing and serving each other. It is very important to stay in the heart.

ASTROLOGICAL INFLUENCE
The corresponding zodiac sign of the Sun is Leo. Therefore, you should be loving, optimistic, and have integrity. Avoid egotism, and don't be too forceful or temperamental.

2 — THE HIGH PRIESTESS

Fluctuation and change. Duality; strife; enmity; dissension; loss by women; perception of high truths. Female principle; directing will; division of fortune.

INFLUENCE ON RELATIONSHIP
See God in your partner and positively direct your emotions to strengthen your spiritual stamina. Do not be overly sensitive, emotional or unrealistically demanding. Develop self-confidence. Stay away from negativity and remain connected to God.

PLANETARY INFLUENCE
A relationship with this vibration is ruled by the Moon, which stimulates the sensitivity in one or both partners. The best way to deal with this is to try not to let one's emotional sensitivity get in the way. This couple would benefit by sharing feelings.

ASTROLOGICAL INFLUENCE
The Moon rules the astrological sign Cancer. You need to practice kindness and compassion. Avoid being overprotective or immoral. Try not to be overemotional.

3 — THE EMPRESS

Harmony; perfection in love; partnership; fruitfulness; action; beauty; happiness; success; luxury. Intuitive and extra-sensory skills, healing, inner balance, self-confidence. Marriage; understanding; conception; protection.

INFLUENCE ON RELATIONSHIP
Avoid unnecessary quarrels. You need to think constructively and balance the relationship by playing together and having fun. It is important to support each other emotionally. Be flexible and positive. Respect your partner by controlling your temper and avoid being dictatorial. Give her or him space when needed.

PLANETARY INFLUENCE
A relationship with this vibration is ruled by Jupiter and would benefit from learning not to be too critical or judgmental of each other. Spend time enjoying fine dining together. To keep the harmony, learning how to cook well will be very important.

ASTROLOGICAL INFLUENCE
Jupiter rules Sagittarius and Pisces. Therefore, stay optimistic, generous and compassionate. A spiritual discipline will be very helpful. Avoid carelessness and lawlessness. Practice tactful communication and stay open-minded. Balance your mood swings. Be careful of escapism.

4 — THE EMPEROR

Initiative. Discoverer. Need of protection. Ambition. Accomplishment; stability; establishment; fixity; endurance; realization; conquest; strife. Creative wisdom. Justice; mental strength; audacity.

INFLUENCE ON RELATIONSHIP
Loyalty and trust are necessary for this union to experience stability and balance. Do not force your ideas. Take the time to listen to your partner. You must develop an uncritical nature. Learn to appreciate each other and work together. Keep fear out of the relationship.

PLANETARY INFLUENCE
A relationship with this vibration is ruled by Uranus. This relationship would benefit from open and honest communication. Practice listening and avoid being too outspoken.

ASTROLOGICAL INFLUENCE
Although 4 is ruled by Uranus, in practical numerology, it is associated with the number 1. The number 1 is the positive aspect of the Sun on the physical plane, whereas 4 is the negative aspect of the Sun on the spiritual plane. The corresponding zodiac sign of the Sun is Leo. Therefore, be loving, optimistic, and have integrity. Avoid egotism, and don't be too forceful or temperamental.

5—THE HEIROPHANT

The teacher, spiritual master or advisor. Inner guidance, highest transformation and divine wisdom. Spirituality. Competition; pain; mental and nervous strain; unfortunate impulses; anger. Manifestation. Will; fight for life; pentagram; protection of belongings.

INFLUENCE ON RELATIONSHIP
Be very honest, respectful and patient with your partner. Stop hurrying. Create time for exercise and relaxation. Traveling will nurture this union. You will be teachers to each other. Maintain your natural sense of humor.

PLANETARY INFLUENCE
A relationship with this vibration is ruled by Mercury. A couple with this vibration should avoid tension and learn how to relax together. Traveling together will be very beneficial.

ASTROLOGICAL INFLUENCE
Mercury rules the astrological signs Gemini and Virgo. Be creative and practice versatility. Keenness will be very helpful. Be simple and straight. Avoid instability, shallowness and overanalysis. Don't give into fault-finding, pettiness and cynicism.

6 — LOVERS

Consciousness through relationship. Love, union of opposites through love, attraction, partnership, connection. Possible uncertainty in marriage; danger of seduction; irregularities; power and action from inspiration. Equilibrium; choice.

INFLUENCE ON RELATIONSHIP
Practice forgiveness and interact pleasantly with your partner. Avoid arguments. Do not engage in intimate relationships outside of your union. Do not tax your nervous system by focusing upon unpleasant events from the past. You may suffer deep disappointment if you are looking for the ideal mate.

PLANETARY INFLUENCE
A relationship with this vibration is ruled by Venus, which brings out one's emotions. This couple would benefit from romantic things, such as flowers and romantic excursions, as well as staying emotionally balanced.

ASTROLOGICAL INFLUENCE
Venus rules the astrological signs Taurus and Libra. Be loyal and reliable. Bring harmony and romance into this relationship. Jealousy, stubbornness and hedonism can be destructive. Avoid indecisiveness.

7 — THE CHARIOT

Triumph; honor; glory; reputation; success though not always enduring; victory; health. Spiritual path. Advice.

INFLUENCE ON RELATIONSHIP
Be open to your partner's way of thinking. Treat your partner with respect and interact peacefully. Do not exhaust yourself by overworking, otherwise you will not have time to nurture your union. Beware of unrealistic expectations.

PLANETARY INFLUENCE
A relationship with this vibration, which is ruled by Neptune, will benefit from spirituality and meditating together. It is important to stay in the heart. Avoid destructive forms of escapism and don't be overly philosophical.

ASTROLOGICAL INFLUENCE
Although 7 is ruled by Neptune, in practical numerology, it is associated with the number 2. The number 2 is the feminine aspect of the Moon on the physical plane, whereas 7 is the masculine aspect of the Moon on the spiritual plane. The corresponding zodiac sign of the Moon is Cancer. Avoid being too mental, and bring your heart into this relationship. Stay grounded in reality. You need to practice kindness and compassion.

8 — STRENGTH

Mental strength is needed to overcome old fears and conditioning, which are responsible for some of the obstacles this vibration brings. Moral liabilities; ruptures; separation; breaking of ties; dissolution; lawsuits. You must create balance by integrating your angelic and animalistic sides. Justice; discipline; karma.

INFLUENCE ON RELATIONSHIP
You must trust your partner and communicate clearly. Avoid engaging in arguments. You may have a tendency to take things too seriously, so learn to smile and have fun with your partner. Take time to relax together. Be friendly and tolerant. Keep fear out of the relationship. Devote time to spirituality.

PLANETARY INFLUENCE
A relationship with this vibration, which is ruled by Saturn, must be very spiritual. Both partners should be understanding and exercise discipline. Practice flexibility in order to avoid frustration. Keep a positive mental attitude.

ASTROLOGICAL INFLUENCE
Saturn rules the astrological signs Capricorn and Aquarius. Be friendly and considerate, and practice patience with your partner. Avoid isolation and passivity. You must respect each other. Avoid getting involved with lovers outside your union. Traveling with your partner will be helpful. Devote time for spiritual growth. Avoid arguments and don't be too unpredictable.

9 — THE HERMIT

Authority and power due to merit; acquisition of experience; wisdom sought for and obtained from above; divine inspiration. A need to seek in silence. Introspection. The wise guide. Satisfaction is finding one's own light and inner wisdom, not in following the masses. Caution; hidden things.

INFLUENCE ON RELATIONSHIP
Avoid any kind of negative communication. Be tolerant with your partner and avoid vengeful thoughts. Keep anger out of this relationship. Turn aggression into cooperation. Maintain your sense of humor.

PLANETARY INFLUENCE
A relationship with this vibration is ruled by Mars. You will benefit from being patient and learning how to be neutral. Avoid outbursts of anger and being overly domineering.

ASTROLOGICAL INFLUENCE
Mars rules the astrological signs Aries and Scorpio. There will be a lot of energy available in this relationship. Practice enthusiasm. Avoid jealousy and vindictiveness. Control all impulsive behavior, and don't be selfish.

10 — WHEEL OF FORTUNE

Elevation from a humble position, or fall from a high position; reversals; auguries; future events; good fortune and happiness (within bounds). Unexpected fortune, expansion, creativity, self-realization. Fluctuation of fortune.

INFLUENCE ON RELATIONSHIP
You can create a beautiful union by being kind to your partner. Avoid criticism, exercise tolerance and speak from your heart. Do not judge your partner too harshly. Work with your partner—not against. Be courteous and helpful. Do not try to dominate each other.

PLANETARY INFLUENCE
A relationship with this vibration is ruled by the Sun, therefore it is best to bring in the qualities of the Sun. This relationship would benefit from sharing and serving each other. It is very important to stay in the heart.

ASTROLOGICAL INFLUENCE
The corresponding zodiac sign of the Sun is Leo. Therefore, you need to be loving, optimistic, and have integrity. Avoid egotism, and don't be too forceful or temperamental.

11 — JUSTICE

Warning of hidden danger; success in some bold enterprises; courage; decision; energy; fortitude. It is necessary to keep the aura strong. Balance, equilibrium and justice. Transformation; spiritual power; the will; innovation; strength to overcome obstacles; meditation.

INFLUENCE ON RELATIONSHIP
Your partner will mirror back to you what you give, therefore be very positive and supportive. You must be kind-hearted and patient. Be gentle, caring and loving. Treat your union as sacred. Do not make false promises or humiliate your partner. Be honest and fair.

PLANETARY INFLUENCE
A relationship with this vibration is ruled by the Moon, which stimulates the sensitivity in one or both partners. The best way to deal with this is to try not to let one's emotional sensitivity get in the way. This couple would benefit by sharing feelings.

ASTROLOGICAL INFLUENCE
The Moon rules the astrological sign Cancer. You need to practice kindness and compassion. Avoid being overprotective or immoral. Try not to be overemotional.

12 — THE HANGED MAN

Surrender to the higher Self and learn to see new ways to avoid becoming stuck. Necessity to break through old behavior patterns and rigid ideologies. Avoid guilt. Be careful of hidden negative influences. Avoid life-threatening adventures. You may be negatively used by others. Enforced sacrifice. One must develop patience and mental strength to face the oppositions of life; desire for liberation.

INFLUENCE ON RELATIONSHIP
Be optimistic and cheerful with your partner. Learn to share meaningfully. Have fun and enjoy each other's company. Avoid anything in the relationship that may cause you mental and emotional stress. Control your temper and anger. Respect your partner. Take relaxing trips together. Do not make promises that you cannot keep.

PLANETARY INFLUENCE
A relationship with this vibration is ruled by Jupiter and would benefit from learning not to be too critical or judgmental of each other and to spend time enjoying fine dining together. To keep the harmony, learning how to cook well will be very important.

ASTROLOGICAL INFLUENCE
Jupiter rules Sagittarius and Pisces. Therefore, stay optimistic, generous, and compassionate. A spiritual discipline will be very helpful. Avoid carelessness and lawlessness. Practice tactful communication and stay open-minded. Balance your mood swings. Be careful of escapism.

13 — DEATH

This is a vibration of magical power. Transformation, death and resurrection; letting go. Ambitions and hopes deceived; sometimes destruction; a number of upheavals; undoing; new beginnings. Symbol of power that needs to be properly used in order to avoid self-destruction.

INFLUENCE ON RELATIONSHIP
You must create trust in this relationship, opening your heart and expressing yourself clearly. Do not be indecisive. Keep your doubting nature away from this union. Learn to appreciate each other. Respect your partner by not having any sexual relationships outside of your union. Work on developing good listening skills.

PLANETARY INFLUENCE
A relationship with this vibration is ruled by Uranus. This relationship would benefit from open and honest communication. Practice listening and avoid being too outspoken.

ASTROLOGICAL INFLUENCE
Although 13/4 is ruled by Uranus, in practical numerology, it is associated with the number 1. The number 1 is the positive aspect of the Sun on the physical plane, whereas 4 is the negative aspect of the Sun on the spiritual plane. The corresponding zodiac sign of the Sun is Leo. Therefore, you need to be loving, optimistic, and have integrity. Avoid egotism, and don't be too forceful or temperamental.

14 — TEMPERANCE

Balance, transformation and union of opposites. Dangers to the position through lack of initiative and indecision. Sexual energy needs to be directed for creativity in order to avoid destructive impulses. This number is good for dealing with money, but be cautious of hidden risks. Realization. Obstacles; perversity.

INFLUENCE ON RELATIONSHIP
Do not make false promises to your partner. Stay true to your word. Be calm and kind, and honor your partner. Do not push. Avoid stressful situations. Learn to listen patiently. Create an atmosphere of joy and union in this relationship. Be aware of arousing resentment in your partner.

PLANETARY INFLUENCE
A relationship with this vibration is ruled by Mercury. A couple with this vibration needs to avoid tension and learn how to relax together. Traveling together will be very beneficial.

ASTROLOGICAL INFLUENCE
Mercury rules the astrological signs Gemini and Virgo. Be creative and practice versatility. Keenness will be very helpful. Be simple and straight. Avoid instability, shallowness and overanalysis. Don't give into fault-finding, pettiness and cynicism.

15 — THE DEVIL

Perception of deeper essence. Humor, sensuality, sexuality. Fate; the inevitable; dangers to the offspring and troubles in the marriage; luxury; material temptation; sometimes obsession; spirituality is a must; good for money and favors. Collaboration; marriage.

INFLUENCE ON RELATIONSHIP
Try to keep your emotions within limits. Practice tolerance and avoid arguments. Do not open the door to promiscuity, because you may be challenged. Organize your life so you may be more efficient. Maintain a spiritual discipline with your partner.

PLANETARY INFLUENCE
A relationship with this vibration is ruled by Venus, which brings out one's emotions. This couple would benefit from romantic things, such as flowers and romantic excursions, as well as staying emotionally balanced.

ASTROLOGICAL INFLUENCE
Venus rules the astrological signs Taurus and Libra. Be loyal and reliable. Bring harmony and romance into this relationship. Jealousy, stubbornness, and hedonism can be destructive. Avoid indecisiveness.

16 — THE TOWER

Far-reaching inner transformation, healing, spiritual renewal. Destruction of the old to make way for the new. Overthrow; falls. Gives warning of some fatality ahead; deviation from your plans; be cautious. Ambition; courage; fighting. Bad luck; losses; laziness.

INFLUENCE ON RELATIONSHIP
Be positive, open and honest with your partner. Communicate kindly and work together to build a strong bond. It is important to respect and honor each other. Avoid all intimate relationships outside of this union. This energy stands for impermanence in relationships.

PLANETARY INFLUENCE
A relationship with this vibration, which is ruled by Neptune, will benefit from spirituality and meditation. It is important to stay in the heart. Avoid destructive forms of escapism and don't be overly philosophical.

ASTROLOGICAL INFLUENCE
Although 7 is ruled by Neptune, in practical numerology it is associated with the number 2. The number 2 is the feminine aspect of the Moon on the physical plane, whereas 7 is the masculine aspect of the Moon on the spiritual plane. The corresponding zodiac sign of the Moon is Cancer. Avoid being too mental, and bring your heart into this relationship. Stay grounded in reality. You need to practice kindness and compassion.

17 — THE STAR

This is known as the *Star of the Magi*. The eight-pointed star of Venus is the symbol of peace and love. It is a very fortunate number. Inspiration, crystallization, radiance, clear vision, trust in self, cosmic connection. Great ideas; veil lifted; renewed vigor.

INFLUENCE ON RELATIONSHIP
The growth potential of this union is great. Trust your partner, be loving and maintain an attitude of peace. Have fun together. Keep unnecessary stress caused by fear and gloominess out of this union. Do not indulge in arguments. Judging your partner may be the worst thing you do. Give him or her a chance.

PLANETARY INFLUENCE
This relationship is ruled by Saturn, because 17 reduces to 8. You must be very spiritual. Both partners should be understanding and exercise discipline. Practice flexibility in order to avoid frustration.

ASTROLOGICAL INFLUENCE
Saturn rules the astrological signs Capricorn and Aquarius. Be friendly and considerate, and practice patience with your partner. Avoid isolation and passivity. You must respect each other. Avoid getting involved with lovers outside your union. Traveling with your partner will be helpful. Devote time for spiritual growth. Avoid arguments and don't be too unpredictable.

18 — THE MOON

Illusion, burning off of karma, struggle with the subconscious. Crosses in love; false sense of security; unprofitable associations with people of the opposite sex; hidden perils; treachery; error. Voluntary change. Dissatisfaction. Be very cautious in order to avoid deception and betrayal.

INFLUENCE ON RELATIONSHIP
Be honest and let your partner clearly know where you stand to avoid any room for deception and betrayal. Be responsible and direct your energy to constructively see the presence of God in your partner. Remember that any anger or betrayal directed toward your partner is a deception of yourself. This would slow your progress down considerably.

PLANETARY INFLUENCE
Although the tarot card 18 corresponds to the Moon, it reduces to the single digit of 9. In practical numerology 9 is the number of Mars. Therefore, you will benefit from being patient and learning how to be neutral. Avoid outbursts of anger and being overly domineering.

ASTROLOGICAL INFLUENCE
Mars rules the astrological signs Aries and Scorpio. There will be a lot of energy available in this relationship. Practice enthusiasm. Avoid jealousy and vindictiveness. Control all impulsive behavior, and don't be selfish.

19 — THE SUN

The Prince of Heaven. Promises success, esteem and honors. Good fortune; fulfilled love relationships; glory; gain; reputation; happy association. Sometimes arrogance. Also wisdom, spirituality and creative energy. Joy, union, harmony and peace.

INFLUENCE ON RELATIONSHIP
This union can prove very promising, providing that trust and the desire to work together are present. You must be heart-centered and keep destructive criticism out of the union. Bring your emotions under control. Be more forthright. Learn to be more open and sharing.

PLANETARY INFLUENCE
A relationship with this vibration is ruled by the Sun, therefore it is best to bring in the qualities of the Sun. This relationship would benefit from sharing and serving each other. It is very important to stay in the heart.

ASTROLOGICAL INFLUENCE
The corresponding zodiac sign of the Sun is Leo. Therefore, you should be loving, optimistic, and have integrity. Avoid egotism, and don't be too forceful or temperamental.

20 — JUDGMENT

The Awakening. Unexpected elevation. Inevitable decision. Critical self-analysis. Judgment. Discrimination and discernment. Healing; change; end to difficulties.

INFLUENCE ON RELATIONSHIP
Ground yourself and cultivate confidence. Do not allow yourself to undergo frustration. Never lose balance. Be gentle with your partner. Do not let your judgment be colored by your feelings. Do not be too touchy; use your mind to express your emotions in a healthy manner. Do not stuff your feelings inside. Try to avoid petty arguments.

PLANETARY INFLUENCE
A relationship with this vibration reduces to the number 2, which corresponds to the Moon. The Moon stimulates the sensitivity in one or both partners. The best way to deal with this is to try not to let one's emotional sensitivity get in the way. This couple would benefit by sharing feelings.

ASTROLOGICAL INFLUENCE
The Moon rules the astrological sign Cancer. You need to practice kindness and compassion. Avoid being overprotective or immoral. Try not to be overly emotional.

21 — THE WORLD

Crown of the Magi. Synthesis and completion. Dignities; honors; aspirations; success in one's plans after a long fight. Cosmic union, liberation from bondage, burning off of karma. This is a very fortunate vibration.

INFLUENCE ON RELATIONSHIP
Be flexible in your dealings with your partner. Learn to forgive the past and move on. Make an effort to express yourself well. Do not make false promises, because your partner may hold you to it later. Try not to arouse antagonism by being too critical, controlling or demanding. Be more trusting and open. Learn acceptance and remember the power of love.

PLANETARY INFLUENCE
A relationship with this vibration is ruled by Jupiter, because 21 reduces to 3. Therefore, you would benefit from learning not to be too critical or judgmental of each other, and spending time fine dining together. You can promote harmony by learning how to cook well for your partner.

ASTROLOGICAL INFLUENCE
Jupiter rules Sagittarius and Pisces. Therefore, stay optimistic, generous and compassionate. A spiritual discipline will be very helpful. Avoid carelessness and lawlessness. Practice tactful communication and stay open-minded. Balance your mood swings. Be careful of escapism.

CHAPTER FIFTEEN

Planetary Practicum

There are hidden spiritual forces behind every aspect of life. Most of the unseen laws governing our daily lives as well as our solar system have never been explained. In connection with this idea, after years of practical experience and careful investigation, I have found that fate uses the most challenging planets known to the entire spiritual kingdom as its instrument. In numbers they are: 4 (Uranus), 8 (Saturn), and/or 9 (Mars).

As we learned in Chapter 13: Kabbalah and Relationships, Mars (9) is governed by the Lord of War, and Saturn (8) by the Lord of Karma. The appearance of these numbers under certain conditions, such as the waning moon, is a warning sign that is not to be ignored, and action must be taken to avert their fatalistic tendencies. For example, in 1996, the NY-Paris TWA flight 800 (reduces to 8) exploded on July 17 (reduces to 8). In 1999, the NY-Cairo Egypt Air flight 990 (reduces to 9) crashed on October 31 (reduces to 4) during the waning moon.

With regard to Uranus, no one today can plead ignorance of the missing 13th floor in most buildings and especially the fear of Friday the 13th. With closer examination, we realize that 13 reduces to the single digit of 4, which represents Uranus, a powerful planet that invokes mental confusion and disturbance. Uranus (4) is referred to in Indian astrology as Rahu, the dragon's head. It is the other half of Ketu or Neptune. These are the two nodes of the moon, one hundred and eighty degrees apart. Rahu or Uranus (4) brings confusion and drives people toward mistakes.

Most people who live in apartments or houses whose numbers reduce to the single digits of 4, 8, or 9 often experience unusual difficulties in their love relationship, health, or life in general. The influence of these numbers on our lives often seems to be out of our control. They denote hindrances and delays to our plans which can only be conquered through spiritual discipline.

Use the healing mantras *Ra Ma Da Sa*, *Lumen de Lumine* and especially *Triple Mantra*, revealed in Chapter 8 under "Healing Sounds" *(page 66)* to help minimize the challenging influences of these planets, particularly on your love relationship.

Regarding the Influence of the Seven Planets in Relationships

Throughout life, we are all tested by the challenges of time and space. This is as true for love couples as it is for individuals. Although a perfect love relationship without challenges is the desideratum of most people, it is unrealistic to believe that love relationships are easy work. Love partners have to work very hard through their challenges in order to come out strong and victorious. As they recognize and overcome those challenges, they become solid in their union. Challenges are an inescapable part of love relationships, for this is how partners grow and evolve together. Most challenges are so subtle that it is often difficult to identify them. They come to us in various ways. Here are two main ones. First, we can be led astray by listening to the people we love—our family and friends. They in turn may think they are acting and advising in our best interest, whereas they often hurt the relationship as opposed to helping it. Secondly, there are times where our unhealed negative patterns disturb the stability of our love relationship. This process generally happens during the waning moon. Above all, challenges hit the hardest during the periods of Saturn, Mars, Mercury and the Moon.

A person who does not know what to do is at the mercy of whatever life throws his/her way. Let's take as an example the well-known case of President Clinton and Monica Lewinsky to demonstrate the accuracy of this system. President Clinton met Monica Lewinsky within the 52 days before his birthday, while he was in his Saturn period. Through his weaknesses, Saturn caused Monica to become a near-fatal blow to his destiny.

REGARDING THE INFLUENCE OF SATURN UPON THE MONTH AND DAY

August 17 was the worst possible day for Clinton to make his confession on national TV, because as mentioned above, that date fell within his Saturn period. In addition, August is the 8th month of the year and 8 stands for Saturn. When the day is reduced ($17=1+7$) the result is 8. This day had a triple-Saturn impact on Clinton. Saturn, who is the balancer of karma, is also referred to as the planet of darkness. It brings disturbance to the mind, body and spirit, making you lonely and frustrated. It is confining and limiting. Saturn reveals in a hard way what is not working in your life and where you need to change. It can bring humiliation, delays, obstacles, and problems with the law, such as lawsuits.

REGARDING THE INFLUENCE OF MARS

Saturday January 17 was the day Clinton signed the Paula Jones deposition. We find that not only was the moon waning, but also Clinton was in his Mars period. In this system of the seven periods, Mars and Saturn are the worst possible periods to do anything of importance, such as signing a legal document in an unclear manner.

REGARDING THE INFLUENCE OF THE SUN AND CLINTON'S POLITICAL RESILIENCE

The Congressional decision to proceed with the impeachment hearing took place on October 8—two days before the end of Clinton's Sun period. The Sun rules the first 52 days after your birthday. It is a very favorable time for improving your reputation and shining light on all your affairs. Therefore, the Sun was a major factor in elevating Clinton's reputation during this trying time.

The seven planets rule everything and everyone regardless of who they are or where they are at. They are the immutable laws of nature. The main point to remember is that the Sun, Jupiter and Venus are positive, Mars and Saturn are challenging, and the Moon and Mercury are neutral. If the moon is waning, the Moon and Mercury periods become as challenging as Saturn and Mars. In addition, when Saturn or Mercury are retrograding, the Moon and Mercury periods also become as challenging as Saturn and Mars. As another example, if John is in his Mars period and Mary is in her Jupiter period, their love relationship will be tested because of Mars. Similarly, if John is in his Moon or Mercury period while either Saturn or Mercury is retrograding, his love relationship with Mary will still be tested.

It is unusual for both partners in a love relationship to be in the same challenging period at the same time. That only happens when they are born the same day or a few days apart. For example, if Ben and Susanne were born on January 15, they will both be in their challenging periods at the same time. Also, the same is true if Ben was born on January 10 and Susanne on January 15. Since each period lasts 52 days, Ben will be the first to enter the given period and Susanne will follow five days later. In other words, they will both remain in a challenging period for about 47 days.

Often, when one partner is in a challenging period, the other is in a benefic one. If they are sensitive to the underlying currents, the partner in the benefic period can support the other by balancing the energy of the couple.

To illustrate the above, here are some examples of how the challenges affect us. Let's say that John, who is in a committed love relationship with Mary, is in his Mars period while she is in her Jupiter period. Obviously, Mary will be enjoying the positive influence of Jupiter, which stands for prosperity, job advancement, support in one's work and expansion. The influence of Jupiter can even be felt one week prior to its beginning and a week after its end, the reason being that there are years in which our Jupiter period is so strong that its influence expands beyond 52 days. Now back to our example. John is right in the middle of his Mars period, which signifies delays, calumnies, treason, intrigue, anger and quarrels. Therefore, some of John's negative patterns will be affected and his anger will come out. He will appear quarrelsome to Mary, whose work and social life are going well. She will be annoyed by his quarrelsome behavior and miss the true cause. As a result, their relationship will be seriously affected.

This is exactly what happened to two close friends of mine, whose names I will change to preserve their identity. Rose and Martin are two very successful people in their respective field of endeavors. Rose was in her Jupiter period. Not only was she excelling at work, but she also received an award of notable performance and a bonus. As a result, she felt very good about both herself and her work. Her friends and family regarded her with respect and admiration. Everything was going well for her. Martin, on the contrary, was in the middle of his Mars period, which caused his unhealed childhood patterns to come to the surface. As a result, he was upset and quarrelsome. Also, he was often rude in his communication with Rose. She took it personally and moved out of their apartment. Rose was unaware of the impact of Mars. She expressed her discontentment to her close friends, some of whom made the matter even worse by giving suggestions that were unsupportive to her love relationship with Martin. She got more frustrated and became mean and spiteful towards Martin. During challenging periods, couples are very vulnerable. Therefore, anyone in their entourage who gives suggestions which are not constructive and supportive can affect their union. After days of seeing Martin under the mask of negativity, Rose decided to meditate. As a result, she realized that Martin was not the villain or evil person that she painted. She started to see the true Martin—a kind, generous and very intelligent individual, full of love. He was the victim of the impact of Mars. She was able to recall the information from the Kabbalah workshop she took with me. She immediately phoned me to relate that she did not even realize that Martin was in his Mars period. Also, she told me that she felt misled by some of her close friends. My comment to her was that sometimes close friends will help your relationship, and other times, they can destroy your love union. Usually, they are not aware when they do it. Very often they think they are acting in your best interest. Just pray for him and you will help dispel that energy and he will be out of it as if nothing happened. She then decided to use the best defense tool you can find: love. Every day she surrounded and poured love into Martin, being caring and giving. Her tone of voice, her look, everything about her gave love to Martin. As a result, Martin's energy shifted positively.

When a love couple is faced with challenge, the one in the strongest position needs to take the lead and use the power of love to clear the way and restore stability. Any time that a couple overcomes a challenge, their bond becomes strong and pure. Rose was spiritual enough to rise above unsupportive comments from her close entourage. As a result, she was able to turn their challenge around, and they are now very close and happily married. The fact is, darkness cannot stand before the power of love. When the challenging planets are faced with love, they become positive. The friends who were unsupportive to their relationship during Rose and Martin's challenge are now envious of them.

In another instance, a couple I knew was undergoing troubles. In this particular case, Justin was in his Saturn period and Kathy was in her Mercury period. This renders communication very difficult. The same thing is also true for someone who is in his/her Mercury period while Saturn is retrograding. It feels like a wall between two people. One of them completely closes off and cannot hear what the other is saying. This is exactly what happened to Kathy. She was in her Mercury period while Saturn was retrograding. It made it difficult for her to reach the heart of Justin, who was already pursuing another agenda. Justin knew that he was in his Saturn period, a time when nothing is clear. He decided to leave her for a seemingly important job opportunity. Kathy phoned me crying. I quickly charted the situation and told her that he would call her back with a different story within seven months, since such karma is resolved either within seven months or seven years. Sometimes she would call and tell me that she heard that he was doing fine. Other times she would relate to me that he called telling her how happy he was. I finally told her to go beyond the appearances. All of what she was hearing was a false projection of what the situation really was. I also told her that when you work with the seven planets, you learn to see the apple tree in its seed. You have to go to the core of what an event really is. Finally Kathy called me to say that Justin called her in tears. Everything in his life started to deteriorate as soon as he left. He could no longer keep the deceptive appearance up. In fact, he could barely survive. He was completely sorry and wanted to come back. Here we have a typical backlash of a decision taken at the wrong time under the influence of challenging planets. For Kathy, it was too late to re-establish their relationship. Such decisions can sometimes destroy your whole life.

In a third instance, Brian was in his Moon period when he married Maggie, who was in her Saturn period. This happened during the waning moon, which is definitely *not* a good time to bring anything new into one's life, especially a marriage. They were both very spiritual and meditated together. This allowed them to overcome most of their tests for the first six years. During their seventh year of marriage, Brian was traveling a lot because of job opportunities. He went on a long trip during his wife's Mercury period. Mercury can be very deceptive. She engaged in an extramarital affair, which turned out to be a fatal attraction. The man would then call her at home to disturb the peace of her stable relationship. This continued after her husband returned, and then it got out of control. The whole situation made her miserable, broke her husband's heart and tarnished their relationship for good. They ended up in an ugly divorce.

Anytime things go wrong in your life or in your relationship, my advice is to just keep cool. Take a piece of paper and chart the impact of the planets on both you and your partner. It sounds simple, but it works. These planets are the best guide in understanding the situation at hand. Knowledge of the planets is a legacy left to us by the ancient students of nature who had more time for meditation and insight into the laws of nature than we do today in our busy world. Why should we reinvent the wheel? Why not build upon what is already there and take advantage of this free guidance? It has worked in the past, it still works now, and it will work in the future.

One can minimize adversity and misfortune by simply working with the forces of nature, which are expressed by the seven creative planets and the spiritual science of numbers. Life does not have to be a guessing game. When times are unfavorable for you, refrain from making decisions that will negatively affect your whole life. By doing so, you will spare yourself from much unnecessary struggle. It is vital to have a system which allows us to see the unseen and know the unknown in order to gracefully face the challenges of time and space. Until recently, this science had never been revealed to anyone outside a small circle. This knowledge gives you early warnings of pitfalls, so that you may save yourself from unnecessary misfortune or adversity. It is designed to make your journey through life happy, successful and fulfilling.

CHAPTER SIXTEEN

Helpful Meditations

Each of the following meditations or exercises should ideally be done for a minimum of 40 days and a maximum of 120 days to reach the desired effect. Problems are based upon negative patterns of energy. It takes 40 days to change an old pattern, and it takes another 40 days to replace the old with a new pattern. Finally, an additional 40 days permanently seals the new pattern in one's body and psyche.

It is very important to begin your meditation or Kundalini yoga practice by tuning in before you begin. It is also recommended to tune out at the end to consolidate and integrate your energies. Use the *Adi Mantra* to tune in and the *Bij Mantra* to tune out.

TUNE IN: ADI MANTRA

You can quickly center yourself through a few repetitions of the Adi Mantra. It opens the protective channel for energy to flow and tunes you into the Supreme Consciousness. From practical experience, we suggest that you tune in with this before starting all meditations and exercises. Breath gives power to the mantra, so always chant after taking a full breath through the nose.

- Sit either in easy pose with your legs crossed, or in a chair with the feet flat on the floor. The spine is straight.
- Press your palms together in prayer pose, thumbs at the sternum.
- Chant at least three times. Do the first part on one breath (ONG NAMO), take another quick breath and do the second part (GURU DEV NAMO). Feel the sound resonating through your head.

ONG NAMO,
GURU DEV NAMO

This means "I call on the infinite creative consciousness. I call on the divine within." By chanting this mantra, you will be establishing a protective link in the chain of golden light from you to your teacher, who is in turn linked to his teacher and to the Divine Source. This mantra, when chanted in proper consciousness, opens the connection between the self and the divine teacher within. Therefore, you are calling on your higher Self and all other beings of light for guidance and protection.

TUNE OUT: BIJ MANTRA

"Sat Nam" is the Bij Mantra, which means "the name of God is truth," "true identity," and "Truth is my identity." This is a universal mantra whose sound embodies truth itself. It is used to connect with the infinity that is within you. Use this mantra to exit from your meditations.

◆ Place your hands in prayer pose.
◆ Inhale deeply. On the exhale, chant a long SAT and a short NAM.

SAAAAAAAT NAM

MEDITATION: EMOTIONAL BALANCE

This meditation will cool your emotions and bring you back to a calm and harmonious state.

Position:
Sit in easy pose. The left hand is resting on the knee in gyan mudra (thumb tip to index fingertip). The right hand is at the nose, with the fingers together and pointing up.

a) Close the right nostril off with the thumb. Inhale deeply through the left nostril.

b) Use the pinkie finger to block the left nostril and exhale slowly through the right nostril.

Time:
Continue this cycle inhaling left and exhaling right for 10 minutes. To end, inhale both nostrils, hold for a moment, relax and meditate.

Note: Drinking several glasses of water when you feel emotional will also help restore balance.

MEDITATION: ATTRACT THE RIGHT PARTNER

The secret of attracting the right love mate resides in the aura, the breath and self-love.

Regarding the Aura
If you want to attract the best mate for you, focus on your aura. Work on it every day until it becomes magnetic, strong and beautiful. (Refer to Chapter 5.) The magnetism of your aura will do the work of attracting a partner. If he is the wrong one, the strength of your aura will protect you by exposing his hidden agenda. When the aura is strong, it radiates a very powerful light. Where there is light, there cannot be darkness. All that is hidden is revealed under the light. If he is the right partner, then the beauty of your aura will make him feel good in your presence.

Regarding the Breath
If your rate of breath is very fast, you will automatically attract the wrong partner. Why is this? People who breathe very fast generate feelings of anger and nervousness and they tend to be emotional. Therefore, since like attracts like, the person you attract will display those feelings. People who have a slow breath rate radiate peace, love, self-confidence and truth. As a result, they attract such partners.

Here is a simple breathing exercise to practice. It will help elevate your frequency and quiet all commotional emotions and thoughts.

- Sit in a meditative position. Eyes are closed, focused at the third-eye point.
- Inhale 20 counts. Hold the breath 20 counts. Exhale 20 counts.
- Continue for 11-31 minutes.

Regarding Self-Love
Self-love is the root of all love. Until you love yourself, you cannot completely enjoy loving someone else.

MEDITATION FOR MENSTRUAL REGULARITY

KIRTAN KRIYA

This meditation will help re-establish your natural menstrual rhythm after discontinuing birth control pills. It is also an excellent meditation to do for mental and emotional balance.

To prevent getting headaches during this meditation, imagine the energy on each syllable flowing through the crown of your head and proceeding along an L-shaped path toward your third eye.

Position:
Sit in easy pose, spine straight and hands resting on the knees. With each beat of the mantra, touch the thumb tips to the fingertips.

Mantra:

SA TA NA MA

SA	Thumb to the index finger. (Jupiter/Water)	*Birth*
TA	Thumb to the middle finger. (Saturn/Fire)	*Existence*
NA	Thumb to the ring finger. (Sun/Air)	*Death*
MA	Thumb to the baby finger. (Mercury/Ether)	*Rebirth*

Time:
Do this aloud in a normal voice for 5 minutes, then in a strong whisper for 5 minutes, then silently for 10 minutes, then back to a strong whisper for 5 minutes, then aloud for 5 minutes. (Total 30 minutes) To end, inhale deeply and completely exhale. Stretch the arms up above the head and spread the hands wide. Take several deep breaths, then relax.

MEDITATION FOR SYNCHRONICITY

Position:

Sit in easy pose with the legs crossed or in any meditative sitting posture with a straight spine.

Arm and Hand Position: Relax the arms down with the elbows bent. Clasp the hands, palms pressed together and fingers interlaced. Press the right side of the left thumb against the left side of the right thumb and rest the joined thumbs on the index finger which is immediately beneath them. Now raise the forearms up until the hands are in front of the chest at the level of the heart.

The eyes are 1/10th open.

Breath:

Deeply inhale and completely exhale as the mantra is chanted.

Mantra:

Chant the following mantra 5 times in a monotone voice (GURU GURU WAHE GURU, GURU RAM DAS GURU) as the breath is completely exhaled. This repetition takes about 15 seconds:

**GURU GURU WAA-HAY GURU
GURU RAAM DAAS GURU**

Time:

Meditate for 11–31 minutes. This can be practiced at any time.

Comments:

This meditation will totally neutralize the energy flow within the body and build a tremendous protective aura. It brings the mind, body and spirit under control, and enables you to meditate on your own divine force, your own fiber.

MEDITATION: RADIANCE AND PATIENCE

Position:
Sit in a meditative position with the spine straight.

The hands are gently cupped with palms facing upward. Place the right hand over the left with the thumbs touching and pointing away from the body.

The eyes are focused at the tip of the nose, eyelids half closed.

Breath:
Segmented breath-inhale in 4 equal parts. Mentally vibrate the mantra: SA-TA-NA-MA.

Hold the breath and mentally vibrate the mantra 4 times (total of 16 beats).

Exhale in 2 equal breaths mentally vibrating WAHE GURU. WAHE GURU means indescribable ecstasy.

Time:
Continue for 15–62 minutes.

Comments:

The best time to practice this meditation is before bed. If it is practiced regularly, sleep will be deep and the nerves will regenerate. After a few months, the rhythm of your breath as you sleep will be subconsciously regulated in the same rhythm! You will think better, work better, share better, and love better. This rhythmic mantra will eventually progress so that even in daily activities you will automatically hear the mantra and take on the breath rhythm.

Mystically the effect is understood in numerology. The number 11 is the number of infinity in the material world and the conqueror of the physical realm. The number 22 is the infinite number of longing and mastery of the mental realm. The breath is regulated in 22 beats and gives the mind the power to stretch to the infinite.

There cannot be enough praise of this meditation and its growth-promoting effect on the personality. It gives radiance, and the radiance gives patience which is the first condition of real Love. In Love you give without attention to all the mistakes of another as the sun gives light and warmth to all people. The incorporation of this practical universality in the personality comes with the disciplined practice of this meditation.

MEDITATION: CONCENTRATION IN ACTION

If you don't know how to meditate or you want to develop the skill of concentration in action, this technique will help you achieve this. This meditation will teach you how to meditate. It allows you to control your own reaction to any situation and can bring sweetness and one-pointedness to the most outrageous and scattered mind.

Position:
Sit in a meditative position with the spine straight. Feel the pulse on the left wrist with the four fingers of the right hand. Place the fingers in a straight line pressed lightly so that you can feel the pulse in each fingertip. The eyelids are lightly closed.

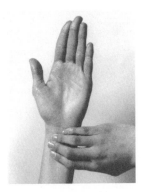

Mental Focus:
Focus your mind at the third eye (the point between the brows).

On each beat of the heart, mentally hear the sound SAT NAM.

Time:
Continue for 11 minutes and slowly increase the time to 31 minutes.

MEDITATION TO NEUTRALIZE TENSION

This is an extremely relaxing meditation. It completely neutralizes tension and puts you in the most relaxed situation you can possibly imagine. By doing this meditation for 40 days, you can completely revitalize your glandular system and establish glandular equilibrium.

Position:

Sit straight. From a relaxed position at the side of the body, bend the elbows and bring the forearms up and in toward each other until the hands meet at the heart level.

Face both palms towards the body and cross the right palm over the left palm with the fingers extended and joined. Place the left thumb in the center of the right palm and cross the right thumb over the left thumb.

The eyes are nine-tenths closed. As the meditation progresses, they may close all the way.

Mantra:

Deeply inhale and completely exhale as you chant the mantra SAT NAM as follows:

SAAAAAAAAAAAT NAM

Time:

Begin with 11 minutes and build up to 31 minutes.

MEDITATION FOR A MAGNETIC PERSONALITY

SODARCHAN CHAKRA KRIYA

Here is a meditation that makes use of prana (life-force) to cleanse mental garbage and purify the mind. Of all the 20 types of yoga, including Kundalini yoga, this is the highest meditation. This is a very powerful meditation for prosperity. It will give you a new start. It is the simplest meditation, but at the same time the hardest. It cuts through all darkness and all barriers of the neurotic or psychotic nature. When a person is in a very bad state, techniques imposed from the outside will not work. The pressure has to be stimulated from within. The tragedy of life is when the subconscious releases garbage into the conscious mind. This meditation invokes the Kundalini to give you the necessary vitality and intuition to combat the negative effects of the subconscious mind.

Position:

Sit with a straight spine (either with legs crossed or sitting on a chair with feet flat on the ground).

Eyes are focused at the tip of the nose, or closed if you prefer.

Mudra:

a) Block off the right nostril with the right thumb. Inhale slowly and deeply through the left nostril and hold the breath. Mentally chant *Wahe Guru* 16 times, while pumping the navel point 3 times with each repetition (once on WA, once on HE, and once on GURU) for a total of 48 pumps.

b) Unblock the right nostril and use the right pinkie finger to block the left nostril. Exhale slowly and deeply through the right nostril. Continue, inhaling left nostril, pumping 48 times, exhaling right.

To end the meditation, inhale and hold 5-10 seconds. Exhale. Then stretch and shake the body for about one minute to circulate the energy.

Time:
Suggested length for this is 31 or 62 minutes a day. The ideal is to start at 31 minutes, but you can begin with 11 minutes, then build up to 31, then 40, and eventually 62.

Comments:
WA means infinity. HE (hay) means identity. The word GURU means wisdom; it is anything that takes one from darkness to light. WAHE GURU means indescribable ecstasy.

    There is no time, no place, no space, and no condition attached to this meditation. Each garbage pit has its own time to clear. If you are going to clean your own garbage, you must estimate and clean it as fast as you can, or as slow as you want. You have to decide how much time you have to clean up your garbage pit. If you can do this meditation for 62 minutes to start with, then build up to the point where you can do it 2 1/2 hours a day (one-tenth of the day), it will give you the nine precious virtues and 18 occult powers. In these 27 total virtues of the world lies the entire universe.

    When practiced for 2 1/2 hours every day, it will make you a perfect superhuman. It purifies the subconscious and takes care of the human life. It will make you extremely intuitive. It brings together all 27 facets of life and makes a human saintly, successful, and qualified. This meditation also gives one pranic power. This meditation never fails. It can give one inner happiness, and bring one to a state of ecstasy in life.

MEDITATION TO ELIMINATE NEGATIVITY AND BALANCE THE EGO

PART A Position:

Sit in easy pose with the spine straight. Tip the chin down into the cavity at the top of the sternum between the collar bones. Hands form the receptive Gyan mudra with the index finger on the tip of the thumb. Bend the forearms, so they are parallel to the ground with the elbows gently resting at the waist. Palms face up.

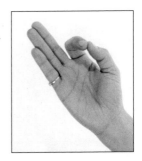

Mental Focus:

Concentrate at the root of the nose between the eyebrows, feeling as if the eyebrows and forearms are in line and the brow extends as an imaginary third arm.

Breath:

Inhale in 4 equal parts, mentally vibrating the mantra SAT SAT SAT SAT. Exhale completely in one long breath silently repeating the mantra NAAM. Continue for 11 minutes. Then inhale deeply and, slowly bringing the neck back with the nose high up, exhale. Straighten the neck to meditate.

PART B Position:

Sit in lotus position or easy pose. Put the hands palms up under the buttocks. The arms go in between the legs, not around them. Drop the head back so the chin is high and concentrate mentally through the rectum.

Breath:

Inhale deeply in 4 equal parts, mentally vibrating SAT SAT SAT SAT. Exhale in one breath, vibrating NAAAM. Continue for 11 minutes.

Then inhale and bring the neck straight, relax the body and the breath completely and meditate.

Comments:

In life there are constantly waves of emotions, yet life is not these waves. The highest point of consciousness in life is love, but love is a constant frequency of vibrations throughout life that has no condition in it. The problem with us is that the positive and negative aspects of the ego are not balanced, so no neutrality and constancy can take root. Positive ego is the constant vibratory projection of the self. The negative ego is the overprojection or undercontraction of the self. The imbalance of these two makes us unable to conquer the fear of death, so we resist changing and evolving to higher consciousness, since every real change is experienced as death. This meditation balances the ego, conquers the fear of death, gives sound sleep, eliminates strange dreams and creates a positive attitude in life. It is especially good to practice at sunset or whenever the sun forms a 60-degree angle to you. These periods of the day are your daily weak points when negativity can easily triumph. This meditation draws out the negativity and eliminates it.

There are two parts to this meditation. "A" is the positive ego stimulant. "B" stimulates the negative ego, and it will sometimes result in depression and very unruly thoughts. The best procedure is always to practice the two parts together. After a slow buildup of time, "A" can be practiced for 31 minutes and "B" can be practiced for 31 minutes. This should then be followed by 11 minutes of deep relaxation.

A faithful practice of this meditation produces a vitality in the etheric body so that it becomes extremely strong and begins to totally regulate the physical glands. This balances the glandular system so that the emotions become constant and the mind becomes divine in its actual potential. The glands will secrete to the total rhythm of the individual psyche rather than from fragmented segments of the self. This new unity is the ecstasy.

MEDITATION: ELIMINATE PHOBIAS & INSECURITIES

SAT KRIYA

This is a fundamental exercise in Kundalini yoga that works on all levels of your being. Its effects are numerous. Sat Kriya strengthens the entire sexual system and stimulates its natural flow of energy. This relaxes sexual phobias. It allows you to control the insistent sexual impulse by rechanneling sexual energy to creative and healing activities in the body. People who are severely maladjusted or who have mental problems benefit from this meditation since these disturbances are always connected with the imbalance in the energies of the lower three chakras. It promotes an overall improvement of health by massaging the inner organs and strengthening the heart through the pumping motion. This exercise works directly on stimulating and channeling the Kundalini energy, so it must always be practiced with the mantra SAT NAM.

Position:

a) Sit on your heels (rock pose) and stretch the arms straight over the head. Elbows are straight and hug the ears. Make sure the spine remains straight.

b) Interlace the fingers, except for the index fingers, which touch and point straight up.

Mantra: SAT NAM

Chant SAT NAM from the navel, rhythmically, about 8 times per 10 seconds.

On the SAT, pull the navel and diaphragm up and back towards the spine. Mulabhand (root lock) will happen automatically when the navel pulls in. On the NAM, relax the belly.

Time:

Continue for 3 minutes, because it takes 3 minutes for the blood to completely circulate through the body.

To End:

Inhale, squeezing the muscles tight along the entire torso, from buttocks up past the shoulders. Imagine that the energy is flowing up the spine and out the third eye. Relax on your back. (Deep relaxation after this exercise should ideally be twice as long as the duration of the exercise.)

Note:

You can build up to 31 minutes, but remember that relaxation immediately afterwards is vital. A good way to build up the time is to start at 3 minutes and rest for 2 minutes. Repeat this cycle 5 times (total of 15 minutes' Sat Kriya and 10 minutes' rest). Then rest an additional 15-20 minutes. This is a very potent exercise, so prepare yourself with constancy, patience and moderation. Respect the inherent power of this technique by gradually building up to 31 minutes. Let the meditation prepare the ground of your body properly to plant the seed of higher experience. If you have no time for anything else, make this meditation part of your everyday practice.

MEDITATION FOR WHEN YOU DO NOT KNOW WHAT TO DO

This is a very simple but powerful meditation when done correctly. It coordinates both areas of the brain, gives you powerful insight, and coordinates the mystery of the spiritual phenomena into the mastery of the physical, mental and spiritual bodies. Though it looks simple, it solves many complications.

Position:
Sit straight, cross-legged or in a chair. Relax the arms down by the sides of the body. Bend the elbows and raise the hands up until they meet at the level of the chest. The fingers of each hand are extended and joined in a relaxed way. Cross the hands with both palms facing toward the chest. One palm rests in the other  and the thumbs are crossed. The fingers point up at a comfortable angle. The position of the left and right hands is interchangeable for this exercise.

Look at the third eye, then bring the eyes to the tip of the nose.

Breath:
Inhale through the nose, then exhale through the nose.

Now, inhale through the mouth then exhale through the mouth.

Next, inhale through the nose, and exhale through the mouth.

Finally, inhale through the mouth, and exhale through the nose.

Continue this sequence. All breaths should be deep, complete, and powerful. When breathing through the mouth, purse the lips almost as if to whistle.

Time:
Start practicing this meditation for 11 minutes and gradually increase the time to 31 minutes. End by inhaling deeply, hold the breath, then relax in stillness. You may want to lie on your back.

MEDITATION TO BUILD TRUST

This meditation affects the element of trust, which is the basis of faith, commitment and sense of reality. It will give you elevation of spirit, so you can stand up to any challenge. It builds and balances the aura from the heart center (fourth chakra) up.

Position:

Sit in a comfortable meditative pose, prefer-ably cross-legged in easy pose or lotus.

Raise the arms up over the head with the palms facing down, elbows slightly bent. Men, place the right palm on top of the left. Women, place the left palm on top of the right. Thumbtips are touching and pointing back. Eyelids are slightly open and the eyes are looking down toward the upper lip.

Mantra: WAHE GURU

In a barely audible voice, vibrate the sound WA-HE (hay) GURU, while clearly articulating each syllable. Each repetition takes about 2 1/2 seconds.

WA means infinity. HE means identity. The word GURU means wisdom; it is anything that takes one from darkness to light. WAHE GURU means indescribable ecstasy.

Time:

Continue for 11 minutes and very gradually build up to 31. To build up the time, increase the meditation by 1 minute every 15 days of practice until you reach 31 minutes. It is very important to respect these times, since this meditation is very potent and its effects extensive.

MEDITATION FOR COUPLES: CLEAR THE CLOUDS

Position:

Sit in easy pose, back to back with your partner. Hands are resting on the knees in gyan mudra (thumbtip to index fingertip). Meditate at the third-eye point.

Mantra: SA-TA-NA-MA

As you chant each syllable, visualize energy entering the top of the head (crown chakra) and flowing through the head in a L-shaped course out through the third eye and projecting into infinity. This energy pathway is called the golden cord. It connects the pineal gland (center of aliveness and higher awareness) with the pituitary gland (center of intuition). *See also Kirtan Kriya, page 166.*

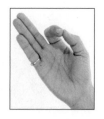

On SA touch the thumbtip to the index fingertip.

On TA touch the thumbtip to the middle finger.

On NA touch the thumbtip to the ring finger.

On MA touch the thumbtip to the pinkie finger.

Time:

Vibrate this in a normal voice for 5 minutes.

Whisper for 5 minutes.

Silently vibrate the mantra for 10 minutes.

Whisper for 5 minutes.

Finally, aloud for 5 minutes.

(Total of 30 minutes)

To End:

Stretch the hands overhead, making the spine long and spreading the fingers wide. Take several deep breaths, then relax.

MEDITATION TO IMPROVE COMMUNICATION

Position:
Sit in a meditative position, with the spine straight and the eyes closed. Touch your right thumb tip to the tip of the pinkie. Do the same for the left side. Rest your hands on your lap. Inhale, and on the exhale chant the following mantra.

Mantra: SA RE SA SA

SA RE SA SA	HAR RE HAR(A) HAR(A)
SA RE SA SA	HAR RE HAR(A) HAR(A)
SA RE SA SA	HAR RE HAR(A) HAR(A)
SARANG	HARANG

Tune:

SA – RE – SA – SA   SA – RE – SA – SA   SA – RE – SA – SA   SA – RUNG
HAR-AY HAR HAR   HAR-AY HAR HAR   HAR-AY HAR HAR   HA – RUNG

Time:
Continue for 11-31 minutes.

Comments:
Adversity cannot stand before this mantra. As humans are the by-product of geography, God is the by-product of human will. We talk to each other through language, just as the Gods talk through their mantras. SA is God. HAR is the Earth. This mantra combines Ether and Earth. It gives you the power of communication; therefore, your words shall have mastery, impact, and shall be vital. This mantra is used to conquer the wisdom of the past, present, and future. Knowledge of the three worlds and all totality will come to the person who recites this mantra regularly.

A PRAYER OF GREAT POTENCY FOR ALL

The quality of your projection is determined by your mental vibration and your spoken words. You can use certain words to raise your frequency, elevate others and heal the planet.

Active blessing is one of the most remarkable ways to uplift humanity. It is also a powerful step toward perfect attunement with the invisible. In reality, the higher powers are deeply moved by the qualities of love, peace and light. Therefore, you can use the verbum to surround yourself with their vibrations, so that you may be protected from unwanted influences.

In connection with the above, the following prayer is perhaps the most profound blessing you can use for yourself and others. It has been empowered in the collective psyche. As a result, reciting it will both nurture your psychic body and allow you to commune with the higher forces of nature in a selfless way. This prayer can be done by itself or as a closure to your yoga and meditation sessions.

If you can, spend a few minutes at intervals every day enveloping yourself with vibrations of love, peace and light. Gradually sense the energy of those words around you and extend it to the universe. Love is the highest vibration available. It turns all misfortunes into delights. Light is the principle of perfection, which brings grace and peace into the life of those who invoke it. Love is the mother of light, and light is the sister of peace. Thus, where there is light, you always find peace. By praying with the trinity of love, peace and light, you are tapping into the principle of the Father, the Son and the Holy Spirit to fill your life with blessings.

In the face of adversity and misfortune, before your fears and insecurities, choose the path of love, peace and light and expand the self to experience your vastness and become victorious. For a life of grace, inflame yourself with this potent prayer and bless humanity, so that we all may regain our rightful place in the celestial hierarchy.

LOVE BEFORE ME
LOVE BEHIND ME
LOVE AT MY LEFT
LOVE AT MY RIGHT
LOVE ABOVE ME
LOVE BELOW ME
LOVE UNTO ME
LOVE IN MY SURROUNDINGS
LOVE TO ALL
LOVE TO THE UNIVERSE

PEACE BEFORE ME
PEACE BEHIND ME
PEACE AT MY LEFT
PEACE AT MY RIGHT
PEACE ABOVE ME
PEACE BELOW ME
PEACE UNTO ME
PEACE IN MY SURROUNDINGS
PEACE TO ALL
PEACE TO THE UNIVERSE

LIGHT BEFORE ME
LIGHT BEHIND ME
LIGHT AT MY LEFT
LIGHT AT MY RIGHT
LIGHT ABOVE ME
LIGHT BELOW ME
LIGHT UNTO ME
LIGHT IN MY SURROUNDINGS
LIGHT TO ALL
LIGHT TO THE UNIVERSE

Praying together strengthens the
love bond and helps minimize conflict.
It brings light into the relationship,
thereby assisting couples in gracefully
moving through challenges.

CHAPTER SEVENTEEN

Helpful Building Blocks to Successful Love Relationships

SELF-LOVE

No one can truly know the reality of love until they start to love themselves. Self-love is the key to a successful relationship, and it is at the very root of lasting love. Those who lack self-love open the door to fear, anger and insecurity. Failure in relationships comes when we act out of our insecurites or neuroses. The truth is, we can never get rid of our destructive patterns until we learn to forgive others and ourselves. We must purify our energies from past negative experiences, so we can move forward and upward. We must embrace and love ourselves without reservation, and realize that each of us is a beautiful ray of the Sun. It is vital to accept, support, appreciate and validate who we are in order to expand and experience our totality. The practice of seeing God in ourselves gives birth to self-love while creating a safe platform for a healthy union. Thus, the God of our heart awakens and helps us overcome any challenge.

RESPECT

A healthy love relationship cannot stand before the lack of respect. Without it, love often falls apart. Therefore, where there is love, there must be respect to bring an atmosphere of sacredness into the

185

relationship. Respect brings out our humanness and elevates the love union.

GRACE

A lovemate should be graceful. Grace bestows a trustworthy presence. Those who have grace are not for sale. Impulsive behavior brings out the animal in us, whereas grace displays our angelic side. Grace causes people to love, trust and value us.

CHARACTER

One of the purposes in life is the development of a strong character. Commitment and consistency are the foundation of character. Those who cannot commit tend to fluctuate like a barometer. When people cannot commit, they show a weakness in character, which reveals a duality in behavior. Duality takes away happiness, and it is very destructive to love relationships.

PARTNERSHIP

Although living together enlivens a love relationship, perhaps most importantly, praying together strengthens the love bond and helps minimize conflict. It brings light into the relationship, thereby assisting couples in gracefully moving through challenges. In addition, compassion, tolerance and loving communication are the keymarks of a healthy partnership. Tolerance makes us non-judgmental, and compassion breaks communication blocks. These qualities allow us to reach our partner's heart.

ROMANCE AND SEXUALITY

Romance adds a healing flavor to the relationship. Without it, the partnership becomes dry. Sexuality should be approached in a very prayerful manner in order to bring out the divinity.

Conclusion

In this book, I have tried my best to demonstrate that through conscious living one can overcome negative patterns and manifest a healthy relationship. The principles revealed in the *Alchemy of Love Relationships* allow you to see the unseen forces directing your relationships, so that you may gracefully face the challenges of time and space. By bringing these divine truths into your experience, they will become part of your knowledge and carry you through any test. Most importantly, they will help your love relationship grow and become unshakable.

Most failures in love unions can be traced to the lack of a spiritual component in the couple's life. The divine spiritual wisdom revealed through the seven creative planets can save you from stressful relationships. Life is a continuous flow within time and space. With the right love mate, the experience of that flow can be graceful and ecstatic.

To my readers, I humbly hope that you familiarize yourself with these principles and apply them, so that you and your mate may grow beautifully in the ecstasy of the light.

The teachings offered in this book are designed to guide you so that you may evolve into your spiritual potentials and embrace your future, while at the same time, remembering your spiritual origin. Understand that the practice of these principles will ultimately lead you and your love mate to a glorious future. They are presented logically so that they are both easily understood and explained. Not only can you apply them to your own life, you can share them with your friends and loved ones, so that they too are able to remove bad luck from their love lives.

The principles revealed in the *Alchemy of Love Relationships* are the divine spiritual wisdom that bestows the spiritual alchemy that transforms lead into gold, negativity into positivity, and darkness into light. They feed the body, guide the mind and nurture the heart by providing understanding and wisdom concerning the essence of a true love union. Its purpose is to give you all the knowledge and power you need to grow and evolve. Armed with this knowledge and power, you will enter into a state of harmony, peace, and divinity that allows you to steer your love relationship in the right direction, thus saving it from dissolution and yourself from exploitation. As a result, you will experience your vastness and come to know the true reality of love.

ABOUT THE AUTHOR

Joseph Michael Levry, also known by his spiritual name Gurunam, is CEO of Universal Force and President of Rootlight, Inc. He is also the founder of Universal Force Yoga and Healing Center located in New York City. He is author of several books, including an in-depth self-study course on the practical application of the sacred science of Kabbalah and Kundalini yoga in daily life. In addition, he is the producer and performer of the *Healing Beyond Medicine* sacred music series.

Joseph Michael Levry is a world-renowned Kabbalist, expert in Kundalini yoga, and the developer of Harmonyum—a transcendental healing system born out of Universal Kabbalah. Since the age of 12, he has been trained in the esoteric arts and sciences and initiated into many spiritual orders, through which he learned the science of Kabbalah. Joseph Michael Levry has illuminated the symbols of Kabbalah and revealed the unifying force of these symbols in his books and lectures, so they may be used to create harmony and peace on earth. Time and time again, he has earned the trust of even the most skeptical people by his precise diagnosis of physical ailments through his well-known unique ability to see and analyze the energy field.

After 30 years of study, research, teaching and travel worldwide, he has created a unique synthesis of the most powerful teachings of Kabbalah and Kundalini yoga to uplift people, help them avoid adversity and improve their lives. He believes that nothing is done by chance, and one can rewrite his or her destiny through the knowledge and application of this divine spiritual wisdom.

Joseph Michael Levry resides in New York City. He holds a Master of Science degree in Industrial Engineering. He currently travels nine months out of the year, lecturing throughout the world, focusing on New York, Los Angeles, Sweden, Germany, the UK and France. He corresponds with thousands of people of every race and religion, guiding them through the process of self-healing, creating meaningful careers, healthy relationships and realizing their dreams.

ROOTLIGHT PUBLICATIONS
HEALING BEYOND MEDICINE SERIES

Books:

Alchemy of Love Relationships
A practical guide to creating successful relationships through the application of spiritual principles from Kabbalah and Kundalini yoga. The application of these principles will completely change your approach to life and relationships. This is an invaluable book for a richer and more fulfilling love relationship.

The Divine Doctor: Healing Beyond Medicine
This book gives you the key to hundreds of mysteries in medicine and healing which are completely unknown within ordinary medical practices, thereby giving you access to timeless healing technologies that are the birthright of humankind. *The Divine Doctor* reveals the precise methods for working with the spiritual body to achieve self-healing and maintain vibrant health. It will also guide you through these techniques, so that you may recover more quickly from illness and become healthy. *The Divine Doctor* is for all yogis, Kabbalists, doctors, serious health practitioners and anyone who desires to achieve self-healing and help others heal through the application of profound meditations and practical techniques. By reading and practicing these sacred teachings, you will nurture your energy, expand your consciousness, purify your mind, and renew yourself.

The Healing Fire of Heaven: Mastering the Invisible Sunlight Fluid
for Healing and Spiritual Growth *(Previously titled The Splendor of the Sun)*
This book will show you practical ways of connecting with the sun in order to capture its many benefits and blessings. Working with the sun is one of the highest, most potent and effective spiritual systems you can come across on this earth. Working with the sun will cause your soul to become active and your spiritual powers to become operative, showing clear visible signs in your mind, spirit and physical body. On a physical level, working with the Sun sparks a complete metamorphosis and renewal of the cells and tissues in the body—all the unhealthy cells and energies are replaced, resulting in health, vitality, complete balance and intelligence.

Lifting the Veil: The Divine Code
Lifting the Veil allows you to penetrate the high mysteries of the Kabbalah by presenting this timeless wisdom in a practical, workable and understandable way. In this book, you will find a time-proven formula to experience a life of grace and joy. Included are over 30 different meditations and simple exercises to enhance your health, balance the mind, body and spirit, and develop intuition.

Advanced Self-study Course (Levels 1–4)
The Sacred Teachings of Kabbalah with Kundalini Yoga

Kabbalah and Kundalini yoga are two ancient and powerful sciences for spiritual growth, and for understanding one's self in relation to the universe. This course is a compelling and extremely practical masterpiece of Universal Kabbalah. The sacred teachings of Kabbalah have been presented in a practical, doable and understandable way. You will be given some of the most effective meditations and prayers that Kabbalah and Kundalini yoga have to offer. The essence of Kabbalah, that was previously hidden and confusingly presented in various books, has been decoded and put into a form that is effective and powerful in its application. By working with this course, all the dormant qualities and virtues in you are brought to full life, resulting in improved health and well-being on all levels. Then your spiritual knowledge, presence and words will start healing and uplifting others.

CDs:

BLISSFUL SPIRIT — Har Gobinday/Ganpati Mantra/Wahe Guru/Ong
These sound vibrations eliminate mental impurities and cause the spirit to blossom, while bestowing divine grace and radiance.

GREEN HOUSE — Har Gobinday (II)/Har Haray Haree Wahe Guru (III)/ Ad Such/*Calm Heart*
These sound vibrations extend the power of projection and protection in the personality. They help open the door to opportunities and attract blessings.

HEALING FIRE — Ong/Prayer of Light/12 Seed Sounds
These sound vibrations give youth, beauty and spiritual illumination. They work on the glandular system and organs. A regular practice of listening to this CD or chanting along with it promotes good health and helps develop intuitive intelligence.

HEAVEN'S TOUCH—Guru Ram Das/Sat Narayan/*Mystical Ivory Coast*
These sound vibrations bring grace, blessings and internal peace. The sound current on the first track synchronizes your energy and expands the aura. It is also for emergency saving grace and spiritual guiding light. The second sound current cleanses the emotions, creates internal peace and allows you to project outer peace. The third track moves you into a meditative space with rhythm.

LUMEN DE LUMINE—For opening the heart and touching the soul
This sound vibration surrounds those who chant or listen to it with a blanket of light. Just listen to it and it will purify and strengthen your aura. Play it in a room and it will clear the energy in a short time. Go to sleep with it and you will wake up revitalized. When faced with challenges, play it continuously; it will eat the darkness out of your life.

MYSTIC LIGHT—RaMa Ram Ram/Hallelu-ya/Lumine De Lumine (II)/ Har Haray Haree/*Sophia*
The sound vibrations on *Mystic Light* revitalize the energy flow within the body and make the aura strong, bright and beautiful. They not only affect the two brain hemispheres and bring you into balance, but they also draw down the protective light and grace of heaven. They give you light, healing, and strength.

OM HOUSE—Activating the Primal Force Within
The sacred sound OM/AUM on *Om House* is mystically vibrated in the most potent and correct way—ONG/AUNG—in order to heal, empower and rejuvenate the chanter or listener. It creates the healing space. This sound is thought to have special universal powers for the creation of worldly things. The divine word OM, which is nothing more than AUM, is pregnant with mysterious power. OM stimulates the psychic centers, and is known to have certain therapeutic value.

RA MA DA SA—To heal and/or maintain balance and health
This sound vibration cuts across time and space and brings healing. It maintains, strengthens and improves your health. It can generate beneficial energy in hospital rooms and places of recovery. It will also create a peaceful and productive environment in the workplace. Families can benefit from its harmonizing effects on the home, children and even pets.

SOUL TRANCE — Wahe Guru (II)/Har/*Love, Peace, Light to All (SaReGaMa)*
These sound vibrations help awaken the soul, so you may manifest your higher destiny. They help give clarity, stability, and harmony.

SOUNDS OF THE ETHER — Ad Such/I AM That I AM/Aim/ Hari Har/*The Fire of Prayer*
The sound vibrations on this CD open the door to opportunity, good fortune and the realization of one's dreams and ambitions. When you chant and/or listen to them, you are calling upon the divine helping hand to assist you in attracting true happiness. As a result, you will be blessed with a fulfilling and successful earthly life.

TRIPLE MANTRA—For protection and to clear obstacles
This sound vibration clears all types of psychic and physical obstacles in one's daily life. It will strengthen your magnetic field and keep negativity away, and it is a powerful protection against car, plane or other accidents. This mantra cuts through all opposing vibrations, thoughts, words and actions.

◆

To obtain our full, updated list of publications and offerings, such as books and meditation/mantra CDs, please contact Rootlight, Inc. by phone, mail, e-mail or visit our web site. In addition, contact us if you would also like more information on Universal Kabbalah workshops, Kundalini yoga and meditation intensives or Harmonyum Healing.

Please visit us at www.rootlight.com for more selections.

Rootlight Order Form

Title	Each	Qty.	Subtotal
Books			
Alchemy of Love Relationships (2004 EDITION)	$23	x _____	= _____
The Divine Doctor (2004 EDITION)	$25	x _____	= _____
Lifting the Veil (2003 EDITION)	$23	x _____	= _____
The Healing Fire of Heaven	$23	x _____	= _____
Advanced Self-study Course			
Level 1	$390	x _____	= _____
Level 2	$390	x _____	= _____
Level 3	$390	x _____	= _____
Level 4	$390	x _____	= _____
CDs			
Blissful Spirit	$19	x _____	= _____
Green House	$19	x _____	= _____
Healing Fire	$19	x _____	= _____
Heaven's Touch	$19	x _____	= _____
Lumen de Lumine	$19	x _____	= _____
Mystic Light	$19	x _____	= _____
OM House	$19	x _____	= _____
Ra Ma Da Sa	$19	x _____	= _____
Soul Trance	$19	x _____	= _____
Sounds of the Ether	$19	x _____	= _____
Triple Mantra	$19	x _____	= _____

SUBTOTAL _____

Shipping in USA:
add $5.50 for 1st item,
$.50 each additional item.

Shipping/Handling _____
N.Y. residents add 8.65% sales tax _____
TOTAL DUE _____

Prices subject to change (8/04)

PLEASE CONTINUE ORDER ON OTHER SIDE OF FORM>>>

(Please print clearly)

PAYMENT INFORMATION:

Payment enclosed: ❑ Check ❑ Money Order
Please make checks payable to: Rootlight, Inc.

Please charge order to my credit card: ❑ Visa ❑ Mastercard

NAME AS SHOWN ON CARD:

CREDIT CARD NUMBER

EXPIRATION DATE MM/DD/YYYY

SIGNATURE

SHIPPING INFORMATION

NAME

ADDRESS

CITY   STATE   ZIP

PHONE OR E-MAIL (if we have questions about your order)

Thank you for your order!

ROOTLIGHT, INC.
15 Park Avenue Suite 7C, New York, NY 10016
TOLL FREE IN U.S.: **(888) 852-2100** FAX: **(212) 685-1710**
rootlightorder@aol.com rootlight@earthlink.net

Please visit us at www.rootlight.com

UNIVERSAL FORCE HEALING CENTER

7 WEST 24TH STREET
NEW YORK, NY 10010
T 917.606.1730
F 917.606.1765
www.universalforceyoga.com

We are a sanctuary dedicated to providing tools, knowledge and inspiration for self-healing and infinite growth.

Now more than ever it is vital to heal yourself. Joseph Michael Levry, Gurunam, world-renowned Kabbalist, expert in Kundalini Yoga and founder of Universal Force Healing Center is fond of repeating: "The only permanent form of healing is self-healing." This is a defining aspect of Universal Force. We are here to be a catalyst for your well-being, health and peace. Our beautiful, bright, peaceful studio receives nourishing energy from the sunlight that pours in from an oversized skylight offering a serene, uplifting and supportive environment in which to begin or expand your yoga and meditation practice. Experience for your Self the deep joy that infuses our studio and enhances your practice.

We are happy to offer:

- UNIVERSAL KABBALAH STUDIES
- OVER 50 YOGA CLASSES WEEKLY
- CHILDREN'S YOGA PROGRAM
- CUSTOM-TAILORED CORPORATE YOGA PROGRAMS
- PRIVATE YOGA
- CONTINUING EDUCATION AND WORKSHOPS
- HOLISTIC HEALING AND MASSAGE
- SPA OFFERINGS
- RETREATS
- YOGA TEACHER TRAINING
- HEALING CIRCLES